MORMONS ARE
BIBLE CHRISTIANS

MORMONS ARE BIBLE CHRISTIANS

H. Kay Pugmire

ISBN 978-1-300-90244-7

Dedicated to:

THOSE WHO LOVE THE TRUTH
AND HAVE THE DESIRE
AND COURAGE TO CHANGE

CONTENTS

ACKNOWLEDGMENTS

There are many people who I would like to thank for making this book possible. The first is my wife, who I believe, was selected by our Heavenly Father as my eternal companion. She has allowed me to share the gospel of Jesus Christ with anyone who would listen, even when the meetings went on for months. Often, when it was possible, she was my missionary companion. Her commitment to support me in this gift of sharing was an evidence of her faith that the Lord would bless us as we served him. "Seek ye first the kingdom of God, and his righteousness; and *all these things shall be added unto you.*" (Matthew 6:33) That promise has been literally fulfilled. She could be considered the co-author for the many hours she has given to bring the book to print.

Our son Jim has read and edited each chapter and made numerous corrections and suggestions. His help was a real blessing, because he had already written and published three books. From the very beginning I asked him if he would finish the book if something happened to me. I feel confident that he could have written this book because of his knowledge of the gospel of Jesus Christ and his unique ability to teach it.

Our son Mark, who also read each chapter, made some valuable suggestions to improve the book. He was aware of the need to clarify what I was writing. He too could have written this book because of his gift for writing and his understanding of the gospel of Jesus Christ.

To Fred Berg and Merwin Waite, who I met at "boot camp" in the U. S. Navy after enlisting at age 17. This was my first missionary experience of sharing the gospel of Jesus Christ. Our teacher was Merwin Waite, who was a gifted Mormon boy from southern California. I was a member of The Church of Jesus Christ of Latter-day Saints (Mormon), but I had never shared what I believe with anyone. Fred Berg was an enthusiastic investigator who attended church with us and accepted fully the gospel of Jesus Christ. We all served full time missions for the church after our two years in the navy and have served full time missions with our wives after our retirement. *It was Fred Berg's idea to write this book.* He asked for my help, but because we both had a different approach, I suggested that we each write our own book.

To Richard "Skip" Christenson, who has shared and supported my missionary endeavors for sixty years. He is responsible for helping create two of the visual aids in this book. "Skip" and I have shared the heartache and the joy of promoting more effective missionary work since we were missionaries in the Eastern States Mission for the Church of Jesus Christ of Latter-day Saints.

To our friend Howard Salisbury who helped make the gospel of Jesus Christ relevant in all we do. He was a mentor and teacher during the early years of our church service. He too could have written this book if he had lived longer. His unique understanding of the gospel and of life is found within these pages. For example, he explained the relationship of faith and grace over 50 years ago.

Finally I would like to thank all those great people with whom I have shared the gospel of Jesus Christ, because we have prayed and learned together and the Holy Ghost was our teacher. Some of your stories are included within these chapters and I wish all of them could have been shared. Your desire to learn the gospel of Jesus Christ and then living it has changed your lives and mine. Your stories and our friendship have become the motivation to write this book. You know that Mormons Are Bible Christians!

This book is not a publication of the Church of Jesus Christ of Latter-day Saints. As the author, I alone am responsible for the contents and I have sincerely tried to conform to the Holy Scriptures.

PREFACE

My name is H. Kay Pugmire; I am a Mormon which is a nickname for a member of The Church of Jesus Christ of Latter-day Saints. I served a two year mission for my church at age 23. That was 60 years ago. Since then I have been teaching the Gospel of Jesus Christ from the Bible to anyone who would listen. That is not how I made my living, but it is how I have lived and what I have lived for. I have sold life insurance for 60 years and that is how I supported my family. Life insurance helps families prepare financially for death and the Gospel of Jesus Christ helps them prepare spiritually. My vocation, in this life, and my avocation have been blended together so I could follow the Savior's admonition: "But seek ye first the kingdom of God, and his righteousness; and all these things shall be added unto you" (Matthew 6:33).

My reason for writing this book is to help change the perception some Christians have about my church. According to a public opinion pollster at the Foundation for Apologetic Information and Research Conference "Sixty-seven percent of Americans are uncertain whether Mormons believe the Bible. Seventy-seven percent of Americans are uncertain whether Mormons are Christians." That is shocking. Are there that many Americans unaware that the fourth largest Christian church in the United States is The Church of Jesus Christ of Latter-day Saints and it is a "Christian church"? These unfortunate perceptions are also a reflection on the failure of our 14 million members to be more visible to their neighbors and in their communities.

I have another reason for writing this book. I have wanted to write a book as a legacy for my children, grandchildren and great grandchildren, even those who have not been born yet. It is my testament to them of what is really important in life–the teachings of Jesus Christ.

So, dear reader, whether you are my family or my friends who I have not met yet, the message is the same. Jesus Christ is your Savior and I hope what I have written will bring you closer to him. I will try to keep it simple, because that's what Jesus would do.

INTRODUCTION

I believe the Bible is the most extraordinary book in the history of this world. This book of scripture contains the life and ministry of Jesus Christ. As "Bible Christians" we believe **"For God so loved the world, that he gave his only begotten Son, that whosoever believeth in him should not perish, but have everlasting life"** (John 3:16). I believe that with all my heart. Mormons believe that along with all other Christians. However, believing in Christ is a starting point. Jesus Christ, our Savior said: **"If ye love me, keep my commandments"** (John 14:15). He also said: **"Come follow me"** (Luke 9:23). Can we truly follow Christ and not understand his teachings? That's why we need to read the Bible and to understand it.

In 1963 I was reviewing the life insurance of a client and his wife, Terry and Jan. Our initial discussion was the financial preparation for death and that led to questions about the spiritual preparation for this traumatic event. Terry was a teacher by profession and he was teaching the youth in Sunday School in the church where he had been raised. He told me he was going to stop teaching that class. When I asked him why he said: "When I was answering the student's questions I was concerned about whether I believed those answers. I was answering from the things that I had learned from my youth and from the lesson material I was given. It was at that point that I began a more thorough searching for truth. Because I wasn't sure of what I believed I felt it inappropriate for me to teach the youth until I had gained a testimony of those things I was teaching."

He resigned because he was not sure the answers he was giving were true. I asked him what he was going to do after he resigned. He said he was going to study the Bible. I suggested that we study the Bible together. We did, and within a few weeks they said they had learned more than they could have imagined. They knew Bible stories, but they didn't know the "Story of the Bible." (That is one of the chapters in this book.) They learned: Where they came from. Why they are here on earth. What happens to them after death. They became "gospel teachers" and devoted Bible Christians.

Jan died a few years ago. I miss the "Thank You" cards she sent on Thanksgiving Day. Terry remains a close friend and misses his sweetheart, but he knows where she is and is at peace because they have an eternal marriage and he will see her again.

In relating this experience, please note that they were already "Bible Christians" before I met with them. They believed along with me and other Bible Christians these common teachings about Christ:

The birth of Jesus Christ. "And she (Mary) shall bring forth a son, and thou shalt call his name JESUS: for he shall save his people from their sins" (Matthew 1:21).

John the Baptist's testimony of Jesus Christ. "The next day John (John the Baptist) seeth Jesus coming unto him, and saith, Behold the Lamb of God, which taketh away the sin of the world" (John 1:29).

The baptism of Jesus Christ. "Then cometh Jesus from Galilee to Jordan unto John, to be baptized of him. But John forbad him, saying, I have need to be baptized of thee, and comest thou to me? And Jesus answering said unto him, *Suffer it to be so now: for thus it becometh us to fulfil all righteousness.* Then he suffered him. And Jesus, when he was baptized, went up straightway out of the water: and, lo, the heavens were opened unto him, and he saw the Spirit of God descending like a dove, and lighting upon him: *And lo a voice from heaven, saying, This is my beloved Son, in whom I am well pleased*" (Matthew 3:13-17).

Jesus Christ is the only way back to the Father. "Let not your heart (his apostles) be troubled: ye believe in God, believe also in me. In my Father's house are many mansions: if it were not so, I would have told you. I go to prepare a place for you. And if I go and prepare a place for you, I will come again, and receive you unto myself; that where I am, there ye may be also. I am the way, the truth, and the life: no man cometh to the Father, but by me." (John 14:1-3, 6)

Jesus Christ chooses his Twelve Apostles. "And it came to pass in those days, that he (Christ) went out into a mountain to pray, and continued all night in prayer to God. And when it was day, he called unto him his disciples: and of them he chose twelve, whom also he named apostles:" (Luke 6:12-13).

Jesus Christ ordains his Twelve Apostles. "Ye have not chosen me, but I have chosen you, (his apostles) and ordained you, that ye should go and bring forth fruit, and that your fruit should remain: that whatsoever ye shall ask of the Father in my name, he may give it you" (John 15:16).

Jesus Christ gives his Apostles the Sacrament to remember him and his Atonement. "And as they (Christ and his apostles) were eating, Jesus took bread, and blessed it, and brake it, and gave it to the disciples, and said, Take, eat; this is my body. And he took the cup, and gave thanks, and gave it to them, saying, Drink ye all of it; For this is my blood of the new testament, which is shed for many for the remission of sins" (Matthew 26:26-28).

Jesus Christ is crucified and tells the thief on the cross that he will be with him in Paradise. "And he (the thief on the cross) said unto Jesus, Lord, remember me when thou comest into thy kingdom. And Jesus said unto him, Verily I say unto thee, *Today shalt thou be with me in paradise.* And it was about the sixth hour, and there was a darkness over all the earth unto the ninth hour. And the sun was darkened, and the veil of the temple was rent in the midst. And when Jesus had cried with a loud voice, he said, Father, into thy hands I commend my spirit: and having said thus, he gave up the ghost" (Luke 23:42-46).

Jesus Christ is resurrected and overcomes death. "Why seek ye the living among the dead? He is not here, but is risen: remember how he spake unto you when he was yet in Galilee, Saying, The Son of man must be delivered into the hands of sinful men, and be crucified, and the third day rise again" (Luke 24:5-7).

Jesus Christ ascends to his Father three days after his death. "Jesus saith unto her, Mary, She turned herself, and saith unto him, Rabboni; which is to say, Master. Jesus saith unto her, Touch me not; *for I am not yet ascended to my Father:* but go to my brethren, and say unto them, I ascend unto my Father, and your Father; and to my God, and your God" (John 20:16-17).

The resurrected Jesus Christ appears to his Apostles. "And as they (his apostles) thus spake, Jesus himself stood in the midst of them, and saith unto them, Peace be unto you. But they were terrified and affrighted, and supposed that they had seen a spirit. And he said unto them, Why are ye troubled? and why do thoughts arise in your hearts? Behold my hands and my feet, that it is I myself: handle me, and see; for a spirit hath not flesh and bones, as ye see me have" (Luke 24:36-39).

Jesus Christ sends his Apostles to teach all nations. "Go ye (his apostles) therefore, and teach all nations, baptizing them in the name of the Father, and of the Son and of the Holy Ghost: Teaching them to observe all things whatsoever I have commanded you: and, lo, I am with you alway, even unto the end of the world" (Matthew 28:19-20).

We have the scriptures to testify of Jesus Christ. "And many other signs truly did Jesus in the presence of his disciples, which are not written in this book: *But these are written, that ye might believe that Jesus is the Christ, the Son of God; and that believing ye might have life through his name"* (John 20:30-31).

Jesus Christ ascends to Heaven and he will come again. "But ye shall receive power, after that the Holy Ghost is come upon you: and ye shall be witnesses unto me both in Jerusalem, and in all Judaea, and in Samaria, and unto the uttermost part of the earth. And when he had spoken these things, while they beheld, he was taken up; and a cloud received him out of their sight. And while they looked stedfastly toward heaven as he went up, behold, two men stood by them in white apparel; Which also said, Ye men of Galilee, why stand ye gazing up into heaven? *this same Jesus, which is taken up from you into heaven, shall so come in like manner as ye have seen him go into heaven"* (Acts 1:6-11).

I join with all other Bible Christians testifying that these scriptures are true. However, Bible Christians need to know more than this. These scriptures lay a sure foundation that I will build on to show what more Christ and his Prophets and Apostles taught that will strengthen your faith and help you share the gospel of Jesus Christ. We need to remember that the best authority for what Bible Christians believed must come from the Bible, first from Jesus Christ then from his prophets and apostles.

Mormons not only believe what is in the Bible, they teach what is in the Bible.

Note: The quotations from the Bible are taken from the Authorized King James Version

Note: Throughout this book I will use: **Bold for emphasis.**

Note: In this book "Bible Christians" has a twofold meaning:

1. "Early Bible Christians" are those who lived at the time of Christ and his apostles and belonged to The Church he organized and followed his teachings.

2. "Modern day Bible Christians" are "Today's Christians" who are unified in believing in Jesus Christ and the Bible, but are divided in their interpretation of what Christ and his apostles taught.

CHAPTER ONE

LIFE AFTER DEATH

One of the most challenging questions for modern day Christians concerns the salvation of those who never heard of Jesus Christ before they died. Neither the Catholics nor the Protestants have a comforting answer for this important question. They are taught that at death we will be judged, and if we believe in Jesus Christ, we go to a place called Heaven. If at death we haven't accepted Jesus Christ, even if we are good, we go to a place called Hell, and we are there forever.

Let me illustrate the problem. Many years ago a Christian convert from Judaism wrote to "Dear Abby," a newspaper advice columnist, about the death of a cousin. She was described as "a devout young Jewish woman" who "died a slow, agonizing death. Everyone remembered her as a person who had never said an unkind word about anyone." Troubled, the writer went to her Protestant minister, hoping to get some consolation and assurance that her cousin was now in heaven. The minister responded: "She is not in heaven because she didn't believe in Jesus Christ." The columnist asked other ministers to respond, but I do not believe it was ever answered. I sent in the answer that should have been printed, but I never received an acknowledgment. I will give you that answer before we finish this chapter.

First, I want you to think about the minister's answer. Did you like his answer? Do you think he was being unkind? Was his answer comforting? Is this the answer a Biblical Christian would give? What answer would you give? The question was from a member of his congregation and I do not believe he thought he was being judgmental. He knew it wasn't what this member wanted to hear, but it was what he believed was true. It was what he had been taught probably in a theological seminary. Now let's make this a little more personal. Do you know of someone who has died, a family member or a friend, who was not a practicing Christian? Have you wondered where they are?

If you have friends who are not Christian, would you tell them they might not be going to Heaven? (You probably would avoid telling them of any other place.) "Bible Christians" teach you must believe in Jesus Christ to be "saved" and to get into Heaven. **Jesus Christ and his apostles answered this important question that has troubled modern day Christians for two thousand years:** How do people receive salvation if they never heard of Jesus Christ during their life on earth? **The answer to this question is found in the following Bible scriptures.**

When Jesus Christ was on the cross, one of the thieves also on a cross near him, said: "Lord, remember me when thou comest into thy kingdom. And Jesus said unto him, Verily I say unto thee, Today shalt thou be with me in paradise" (Luke 23:42-43).

Jesus did not say he would be with him that day in Heaven. In fact, the Paradise that Jesus spoke of is not Heaven. We know this because three days after his death he was resurrected and appeared to Mary Magdalene at the tomb and said to her: "Touch me not; for **I am not yet ascended to my Father**: but go to my brethren, and say unto them, **I ascend unto my Father,** and your Father; and to my God, and your God" (John 20:17).

What do we learn from these two scriptures? Christ and the thief went to a place called Paradise after they died and yet three days later Christ had still not been to Heaven where His Father was. What did Christ do those three days in Paradise? The answer can be found in Christ's own words: "Verily, verily, I say unto you, The hour is coming, and now is, when **the dead shall hear the voice of the Son of God: and they that hear shall live. ...Marvel not at this: for the hour is coming, in the which all that are in the graves shall hear his voice...**" (John 5:25, 28).

After his resurrection, Christ appeared to his apostles. At first they were frightened and thought he was a spirit. "And he said unto them, Why are ye troubled? and why do thoughts arise in your hearts? Behold my hands and my feet, that it is I myself: handle me, and see; for a spirit hath not flesh and bones, as ye see me have." He then ate with them "and said unto them, Thus it is written, and thus it behoved Christ to suffer, and to rise from the dead the third day: And that repentance and remission of sins should be preached in his name among all nations, beginning at Jerusalem. **And ye are witnesses of these things"** (Luke 24:36-48). **His apostles were special witnesses of Christ** and for Christ. They testified of his mission in mortality and of his ministry for three days in the "Spirit World."

The Apostle Peter said:

For Christ also hath once suffered for sins, the just for the unjust, that he might bring us to God, being put to death in the flesh, but quickened by the Spirit: By which also he went and preached unto the spirits in prison; Which sometime were disobedient, when once the long suffering of God waited in the days of Noah, while the ark was a preparing, wherein few, that is, eight souls were saved by water (1 Peter 3:18-20).

Christ said "the dead shall hear the voice of the Son of God" and they did because he went to the "Spirit World," also called "Paradise" and "Prison." Paradise and Prison do not have the same meaning today as they did in Biblical times. They both refer to the "World of Spirits" where everyone goes after death to await the resurrection.

What is preached to these spirits and why? The Apostle Peter taught, **"For for this cause was the gospel preached also to them that are dead, that they might be judged according to men in the flesh, but live according to God in the spirit"** (1 Peter 4:6).

There it is. Heavenly Father loves all of his children and the Gospel of Jesus Christ will be preached to all of them before they are judged. There are not very many scriptures in the Bible about life after death. You may want to ponder and then pray about these scriptures in 1 Peter. By the power of the Holy Ghost you may know the truth of all things. What you have just learned is what Bible Christians knew almost two thousand years ago, but is not taught by "modern Christians" today.

My next quotations may surprise you. They are from interviews with Dr. Elizabeth Kubler-Ross. She was a physician and psychiatrist who was internationally known as an expert and wrote the book *"On Death and Dying."* She did extensive research in the psychological treatment of terminally ill patients. My quotes do not come from her book; they come from media interviews with Dr. Ross. She said:

3

People are afraid of the unknown, and death is, of course, the greatest unknown. But when hundreds of patients, who had never spoken to one another, started to recount identical experiences, I couldn't ignore what I was getting.

Dr. Ross interviewed hundreds of patients who had been declared legally dead and then were later revived. The interviews, she said, produced "fabulous common denominators which you can't deny." She said the revived patients describe the sensation of floating a few feet above their bodies and are able to accurately describe the resuscitation effort.

"This is not just the spooky stories of someone who has worked with too many dying patients," the author of "*On Death and Dying*" said. "It is a good feeling to be able to say after many years that people don't really die." "I don't just believe that. I know, beyond the shadow of a doubt, that there is life after death." "People who are blind can see. Paraplegics have legs that they can move. They have no pain, no fear, no anxiety. In fact, it is such a beautiful experience that many of them resent being brought back to their physical body." (Detroit UPI)

"And not one of those patients was afraid to die again." "Patients who "died" perceived an immediate separation of a spiritlike self-entity from their bodies." "The patients have reported the greatest feeling of peace and ease." "The person's spirit is always greeted by someone very dear to them who had died earlier" (By Bill Mandel, Knight News Service – Philadelphia).

These same experiences are confirmed by Raymond A. Moody, Jr., M.D., who has written the books "*Life After Life*" and "*Reflections on Life After Life.*" Dr. Kubler-Ross wrote the "Foreword" for those books. In part she said:

It is research such as Dr. Moody presents in his book that will enlighten many and will confirm what we have been taught for two thousand years–that there is life after death. Though he does not claim to have studied death itself, it is evident from his findings that the dying patient continues to have a conscious awareness of his environment after being pronounced clinically dead. This very much coincides with my own research, which has used the accounts of patients who have died and made a comeback, totally against our expectations and often to the surprise of some highly sophisticated, well-known and certainly accomplished physicians. All of these patients have experienced a floating out of their physical bodies, associated with a great sense of peace and wholeness. Most were aware of another person who helped them in their transition to another plane of existence…

Dr. Moody will have to be prepared for a lot of criticism, mainly from two areas. There will be members of the clergy who will be upset by anyone who dares to do research in an area which is supposed to be taboo. Some religious representatives of a denominational church have already expressed their criticism of studies like this. One priest referred to it as "selling cheap grace." Others simply felt that the question of life after death should remain an issue of blind faith and should not be questioned by anyone. The second group of people that Dr. Moody can expect to respond to his book with concern are scientists and physicians who regard this kind of study as "unscientific" (Elizabeth Kubler-Ross, M.D.).

Mary Ann O'Roark, a writer for McCall magazine, wrote the following:

Both baffled and fascinated by these accounts (the experiences of Dr. Kubler-Ross and Dr. Moody), University of Connecticut psychologist and professor Kenneth Ring set out to find an entirely new group of people who had come close to death. In a thoughtful and lucid book, *"Life at Death: A Scientific Investigation of the Near-Death Experience,."* he tells of over a hundred cases that he researched in detail in Connecticut and Maine. Ring and his associates collected and verified as much information about these people as possible… In the course of his research, Ring found that his subjects—men and women of a wide range of age, education, background and temperament—all spoke of what he came to call a "core experience," which occurred when they were close to death or "clinically dead." They told of floating up and away from their bodies, of communicating with loved ones who were already dead, of gliding down a dark tunnel toward a lustrous light, of reaching a place they sensed was a threshold but from which they were drawn back, sometimes by a sense of responsibility toward others. ...There was a sense of great comfort and even bliss in which the person longed to remain and whose positive intensity was carried back to affect the rest of that person's life in the "earthly" world. Regardless of what their attitudes had been before—and their religious beliefs varied widely—these people were convinced that they had been in the presence of some supreme and loving power and had been given a glimpse of a life yet to come.

Perhaps the greatest number of medically detailed cases have been quietly collected over the past 20 years by a prominent cardiologist in Colorado. Dr. Fred Schoonmaker is Chief of Cardiovascular Services at St. Luke's Hospital in Denver. Since 1963 he has amassed medical records and case histories of over 2,000 patients who came close to death. Of that number, over 1,400—some 70 percent—reported having near-death experiences similar to those in Ring's study. In most case, Schoonmaker talked with patients shortly after their brushes with death and asked them to describe the feelings they had during this time. Those patients who responded told of experiences that were serene, accepting, joyous; there were feelings of floating, freedom, light; there were scenes of pastoral calm and sounds of affecting music; there were figures of light to offer reassurance and support. And here too was a reluctance to return to life, and eagerness to continue in the beauty of another world. The cases Schoonmaker investigated also represented a wide range of people. And because of the complex and sophisticated equipment use at his hospital to monitor patients' vital signs, detailed physiological information is also on record in many instances.

'Most physicians in this country don't hear these stories,' says Dr. Michael Sabom, assistant professor of cardiology at Emory University in Georgia. 'Doctors don't listen and patients don't tell them. The stories are very personal and hard to put into words, and people are afraid others will laugh at them, so they keep the experience to themselves, sometime for years.' Sabom himself would have been one of the first to dismiss them. 'I read Raymond Moody's book when it first came out,' he says, 'and I was very skeptical. I thought these stories just couldn't be true. But I was in cardiovascular training at the University of Florida Medical School at the time, and routinely dealt with people who were in cardiac arrest, so a psychiatric social worker and I started to check this out for ourselves. Then we started hearing of these experiences–ones that I could match up with medical information right on the spot.' Over the past four years Sabom has investigated the cases of about 75 patients in which serious brushes with death were accompanied by the same sort of experiences. As a doctor with access to these patients' records, Sabom could find no medical explanation for what they said had occurred. Drugs, shock, or irregular body rhythms–these could account for certain aspects of the experiences in some cases, but certainly not in all (Mary Ann O'Roark, McCall magazine, March 1991 pp26-30).

Do you hear religious leaders quoting Dr. Ross, Dr. Moody, Professor Ring, Dr. Schoonover or Dr. Sabom? What they learned about life after death would not be acceptable to those Christians who believed when you die you were judged and went to "Heaven" or to "Hell." All of these people who had died, regardless of their religion, all went to the same place–"a world of spirits," the place Christ and his apostles taught about in the Bible.

I would like to share an experience I had, when I was asked to speak to an elective class at a local public high school. The class was called Cultural Heritage and guest speakers were invited to explain their religion or culture. For thirteen years I spent a day talking to five classes about "Mormonism."

After several years the teacher (who was a Lutheran) asked me this question: "Do you know what my students talk about after you leave?" I had no idea, because I squeezed in everything I could in fifty minutes. She said: "They talk about what you taught them about **'life after death'** from the Bible." (I gave them the same scriptures I have given you in this chapter.)

I should have known this from letters I received from those students, who thanked me for helping them feel better about their Christian faith. Many were struggling with what they had been taught about "Heaven" and "Hell." For the first time in their lives they received answers which neither their parents nor their ministers could give them. (If people can't get the answers they seek from their Christian community, they will look elsewhere.)

This experience with high school students had such an impact on me that from that time on I always taught God's Plan of Salvation starting with "life after death." Death was no longer "the great unknown," or the end of life, rather, it was the doorway to a wonderful reunion with loved ones who have preceded us in death. Almost always when discussing the "the purpose of life," my first conversation is about "life after death." Almost everyone is concerned about death and we have the most comforting and believable answers and they are easily found in the Bible if you know where to look.

At about the same time when I was speaking at this local high school, I learned a friend at work had a young son who was diagnosed with cancer and was not expected to live. I offered to come to his home and visit with him and his wife. My wife and I did this for several months. We taught them God's Plan of Salvation from the Bible, which included where their son would go if he died. We studied and prayed together until they were prepared for their son to live or die and they left it in the hands of the Lord.

When he passed away, I was asked to take care of the funeral service and to speak. I was a little surprised because they had their own church. These young parents wanted all of their family and friends to hear The Plan of Salvation, especially "what happens after death." Their friends were amazed at the peace and happiness this couple radiated. They were at the door greeting everyone. The sorrow and depression, which usually accompanies funerals, was surpassed by their knowledge and understanding. My friend told me he was disappointed when some of their friends did not attend, because they found most funerals very depressing. Later this father found the courage and faith to speak at the funeral service for his own father.

Most of us are reluctant to talk about death or even contemplate it until someone close to us dies. My mother died at age 46. She had a malignant brain tumor which was not diagnosed for a long time. I was 24 years old and serving a two year mission for our church where I had taught the Plan of Salvation to any who were interested. I knew where my mother was and who she was with. She was in the Spirit World and in the arms of her mother and two children who had died in infancy. She was free from pain and enjoying a joyous reunion with those who had died before her. Of course I was sad, but I knew she was happy and I would see her again.

My father passed from mortality just after he turned sixty-five. We had no preparation for his sudden death. I knew I should speak at his funeral service, although it was not the normal thing to do. My two brothers gave the prayers and my sister gave our father's life sketch. I talked about the Plan of Salvation. It was a wonderful and memorable experience for our family. My parents are together again and are waiting for us to join them. Who shall we mourn for, the living or the dead?

With this new understanding about "Life after Death," we can answer some questions which now might be asked. What is a spirit? Where is this Spirit World? How long will spirits be there?

The spirit is who we really are and is in a likeness to our mortal body without the mortal frailties and imperfections. It is a spirit body with the same gender as the mortal body. The Spirit World is here on earth and righteous spirits will be resurrected at the Second Coming of Christ.

The Apostle Paul taught us about the Second Coming of Jesus Christ and the resurrection of those in the Spirit World:

But I would not have you to be ignorant, brethren, concerning them which are asleep, (dead) that ye sorrow not, even as others which have no hope. For if we believe that Jesus died and rose again, even so them also which sleep in Jesus (those who accept him in mortality or the spirit world) will God bring with him. For this we say unto you by the word of the Lord, that we which are alive and remain unto the coming of the Lord shall not prevent them which are asleep.(dead) For the Lord himself shall descend from heaven with a shout, with the voice of the archangel, and with the trump of God: and the dead in Christ shall rise first: Then we which are alive (at his coming) and remain shall be caught up together with them in the clouds, to meet the Lord in the air: and so shall we ever be with the Lord. Wherefore comfort one another with these words (1 Thessalonians 4:13-18).

Bible Christians believed in the Second Coming of Christ and Mormons share that belief. From the above scripture we learn those who have died will remain in the "Spirit World" until they are resurrected. Everyone will be resurrected and leave the "Spirit World," but there is an order in the resurrection which I will discuss in another chapter.

I hope this chapter on "Life after Death" will be helpful in overcoming any fear you have about death and dying. The early Christians (Bible Christians), who were members of the Church of Jesus Christ, were witnesses of his literal resurrection. Knowledge of Christ's resurrection prepared them for their own deaths, and indeed many of the early Bible Christians gave their lives for their belief in Jesus Christ and his gospel. Today we are not often asked to die because we believe in Jesus Christ, but we are asked to live Christian lives as an example for others.

It is my hope you now share in an understanding about death and it will be renewed each time a loved one passes on. Most Mormon funerals are uplifting and comforting because the fear of death is removed for those who are listening. As the Savior said: **"Peace I leave with you, my peace I give unto you: not as the world giveth, give I unto you. Let not your heart be troubled, neither let it be afraid"** (John 14:27).

After reading this chapter, you might contemplate these questions:

1. What have I learned from the Bible, after reading this chapter, that I didn't know before?

2. How will this new knowledge help me to become a better Christian? The Savior said: "come follow me"–is this path a little clearer now?

3. Do you know someone who needs to know what you have learned, so they too can become a better Christian? For example: Who do I know who is burdened with grief over losing a loved one?

4. Are you comfortable with a belief in a "final" judgment at death where the only two places to go are Heaven, where we will live eternally with God and Christ, or Hell, where we will be in eternal torment living with Satan and the evil spirits who followed him.? What if we are talking about

the death of someone who never had the opportunity to hear about Jesus Christ?

5.   Do you believe what Dr. Elizabeth Kubler-Ross found out, after interviewing hundreds of patients who died? "That people don't really die." "There is life after death." "They have no pain, no fear, no anxiety." "Not one of those patients was afraid to die again." "The person's spirit is always greeted by someone very dear to them who had died earlier." Do you know someone who needs to hear this? As a Christian don't you have a responsibility to share this comforting doctrine from the Bible?

6.   It may surprise you to discover Mormons teach many important gospel principles which have been lost or changed since Biblical times. Those necessary principles are in the following chapters of this book.

7.   You may want to ask some of these same questions as you read the other chapters.

CHAPTER TWO

OUR PRE-MORTAL EXISTENCE

We have reviewed the Bible scriptures about life after death and hopefully this has helped remove the fear of death. We have discovered our spirit is who we really are. We are eternal beings. Therefore we, as spirits, will never die. We will only be separated from our temporary mortal bodies and move on to the next stage of our eternal progression.

Did mortal parents create this spirit body that will never die? We obtained our mortal bodies from earthly parents. Where did our spirit come from? The Apostle Paul said: "Furthermore we have had fathers of our flesh which corrected us, and we gave them reverence: shall we not much rather be in subjection unto **the Father of Spirits**, and live?" (Hebrews 12:9).

Jesus Christ gave us this great example of how to pray and who to pray to: **"After this manner therefore pray ye: Our Father which art in heaven..."** (Matthew 6:9).

Christ, after his resurrection, told Mary Magdalene "...go to my brethren, and say unto them, **I ascend unto my Father, and your Father**; and to my God, and your God" (John 20:17). **Christ's Father in Heaven is also our Father in Heaven. We are His children.**

When the Apostle Paul was teaching the Greeks who God was, he said: "For in him we live, and move, and have our being; as certain also of your own poets have said, **For we are also his offspring**. Forasmuch then **as we are the offspring of God**, we ought not to think that the Godhead is like unto gold, or silver, or stone, graven by art and man's device" (Acts 17:28-29).

I want to share an experience I had when I was on my mission in Wilmington, Delaware in 1954. This is from my journal. "We met an unusual lady who had a note on her door listing all the things she didn't need–peddlers, solicitors, etc. As we spoke with her, **she told**

us her beloved grandmother had died and had repeatedly appeared to her since then. We told her we would like to meet with her and explain why she was having these experiences. She told us she hadn't thought about religion for a long time." After meeting and discussing what we believe about "life after death" and about our relationship with God, she wrote the following prayer:

Heavenly Father
Help me when I try to pray. Help me learn the words to say.
Help me do it every day. Help me, Father, learn to pray.
Help me find that which I seek. Help me all your laws to keep.
Help me, Father, learn to pray. Help me do it every day.
Let me ever thankful be. For all the blessings given me;
Bless those who were sent by thee. As they have also helped me see.
Temptations in my way are placed. That every day they must be faced.
But if I always keep my faith. In you I feel my hope is safe.
I thank you Lord – You helped me pray,
I feel you helped me when I say,
'I now can do it every day. I'm not ashamed, I now can pray.'

This was Bessie Skelly's first prayer, but not her last one.

We don't remember our pre-mortal life, but we often have experiences here that seem familiar to us. I am not talking about reincarnation–I am talking about the eternal progression of God's literal children. We are His children: therefore we are all brothers and sisters.

The Bible teaches this great truth that can change people's lives. It has been my experience that a knowledge of who we are changes us. It changes all our relationships, including our relationship with our Heavenly Father and therefore, our prayers with Him. Bessie Skelly was changed forever after learning her true relationship with her Heavenly Father. She remained a faithful member of the church, serving others until she passed away.

Ponder this teaching of Paul the apostle as he was teaching who God is:

God that made the world and all things therein, seeing that he is Lord of heaven and earth, dwelleth not in temples made with hands;… And hath made of one blood all nations of men for to dwell on all the face of the earth, **and hath determined the times before appointed, and the bounds of their habitation;** (Acts 17:24, 26).

14

Our Heavenly Father determined the time and the place His spirit children would be born on this earth. We are born here at a time and place consistent with the decisions we made when we lived in Heaven.

Now, you might be wondering why you haven't been taught this before, and you may be wondering if there are more scriptures in the Bible that confirm a pre-mortal life. The prophet Jeremiah in the Old Testament didn't remember his pre-mortal life with God, but it was revealed to him by his Father in Heaven. **"Then the word of the LORD came unto me, saying, Before I formed thee in the belly I knew thee; and before thou camest forth out of the womb I sanctified thee, and I ordained thee a prophet unto the nations"** (Jeremiah 1:4-5).

Jeremiah was foreordained to be a prophet unto the nations of the earth, because God **knew him** before his mortal birth. God, our Eternal Father, determined the time and place he would be born (Acts 17:26).

Before this earth was created, Jesus was foreordained to be the Savior. The Apostle Peter taught: "But with the precious blood of Christ, as of a lamb without blemish and without spot: **Who verily was foreordained before the foundation of the world**, but was manifest in these last times for you,..." (1 Peter 1:19-20).

Christ was foreordained for even more than his Atonement. Do you know what his role was in the Creation? "And God said, Let **us** make man in **our** image, after **our** likeness" (Genesis 1:26). Who is God speaking to? Who is "us?"

The Apostle Paul gave the answer: "GOD, who at sundry times and in divers manners spake in time past unto the fathers by the prophets, Hath in these last days spoken unto us by his Son, **whom he hath appointed heir of all things, by whom also he made the worlds;** Who being the brightness of his glory, and the express image of his person, and upholding all things by the word of his power, when he had by himself purged our sins, sat down on the right hand of the Majesty on high; Being made so much better than the angels, as he hath by inheritance obtained a more excellent name than they" (Hebrews 1:1-4).

The creator is Jesus Christ under the direction of His Father. The Father and the Son are two separate persons. We can confirm their role in the Creation from Paul's letter to the saints at Colosse:

Giving thanks unto the Father, which hath made us meet to be partakers of the inheritance of the saints in light: Who hath delivered us from the power of darkness, and hath translated us into the kingdom of his dear Son: In whom we have redemption through his blood, even the forgiveness of sins: Who is the image of the invisible God, the firstborn of every creature: **For by him were all things created,** that are in heaven, and that are in earth, visible and invisible, whether they be thrones, or dominions, or principalities, or powers: **all things were created by him, and for him:** And he is before all things, and by him all things consist. And he is the head of the body, the church: who is the beginning, the firstborn from the dead; that in all things he might have the preeminence. **For it pleased the Father that in him should all fullness dwell;** (Colossians 1:12-19).

Before the creation of this earth there was an important event in Heaven which had a profound effect upon all of God's children who would come to earth. The Apostle John said:

And there was war in heaven: Michael and his angels fought against the dragon; and the dragon fought and his angels, And prevailed not; neither was their place found any more in heaven. And the great dragon was cast out, that old serpent, called the Devil, **and Satan, which deceiveth the whole world: he was cast out into the earth,** and his angels were cast out with him. And I heard a loud voice saying in heaven, Now is come salvation, and strength, and the kingdom of our God, and the power of his Christ: for the accuser of our brethren is cast down, which accused them before our God day and night. And they overcame him by the blood of the Lamb, and by the word of their testimony; and they loved not their lives unto the death. Therefore rejoice, ye heavens, and ye that dwell in them. Woe to the inhabiters of the earth and of the sea! for the devil is come down unto you, having great wrath, because he knoweth that he hath but a short time (Revelation 12:7-12).

This conflict in Heaven (War in Heaven) is not clearly understood by many modern day Christians. The Prophet Isaiah spoke of it:

How art thou fallen from heaven, O Lucifer, son of the morning! how art thou cut down to the ground, which didst weaken the nations! For thou hast said in thine heart, I will ascend into heaven, **I will exalt my throne above the stars of God**: I will sit also upon the mount of the congregation, in the sides of the north: I will ascend above the heights of the clouds; **I will be like the most High**. Yet thou shalt be brought down to hell, to the sides of the pit. They that see thee shall narrowly look upon thee, and consider thee, saying, Is this the man that made the earth to tremble, that did shake kingdoms; That made the world as a wilderness, and destroyed the cities thereof; that opened not the house of his prisoners? (Isaiah 14:12-17).

Those two scriptures in Isaiah and the Book of Revelation are about 700 years apart. They both came by way of revelation from God through the Holy Ghost. It is surprising we don't have much more about this important event. We do have this from the Apostle Peter: "For if God spared not the angels that sinned, but cast them down to hell, and delivered them into chains of darkness, to be reserved unto judgment;" (2 Peter 2:4).

And this from the Book of Jude verse 6: "**And the angels which kept not their first estate**, but left their own habitation, he hath reserved in everlasting chains under darkness unto the judgment of the great day."

Who are these "angels who kept not their first estate?" They are the evil spirits whom Christ and his apostles contended with. I am going to give you some of those scriptures, not to frighten you, but to confirm the reality of evil spirits who were cast out of heaven:

When the even was come, they brought unto him (Jesus) many that were **possessed with devils: and he cast out the spirits** with his word, and healed all that were sick: (Matthew 8:16).

And when he was come to the other side into the country of the Gergesenes, there met him **two possessed with devils**, coming out of the tombs, exceeding fierce, so that no man might pass by that way. And, behold, they cried out, saying, **What have we to do with thee, Jesus, thou Son of God?** art thou come hither to torment us before the time? (Matthew 8:28-29).

And when he (Jesus) had called unto him his twelve disciples, **he gave them power against unclean spirits, to cast them out**, and to heal all manner of sickness and all manner of disease (Matthew 10:1).

And they were astonished at his (Jesus) doctrine: for he taught them as one that had authority, and not as the scribes. And there was in their synagogue **a man with an unclean spirit; and he cried out, Saying, Let us alone; what have we to do with thee, thou Jesus of Nazareth? art thou come to destroy us? I know thee who thou art, the Holy One of God**. And Jesus rebuked him, saying, Hold thy peace, and come out of him. And when the unclean spirit had torn him, and cried with a loud voice, he came out of him. And they were all amazed, insomuch that they questioned among themselves, saying, What thing is this? what new doctrine is this? **for with authority commandeth he even the unclean spirits, and they do obey him** (Mark 1:22-27).

And these signs shall follow them that believe; In my name shall they cast out devils; they shall speak with new tongues; They shall take up serpents; and if they drink any deadly thing, it shall not hurt them: they shall lay hands on the sick, and they shall recover (Mark 16:17-18).

And God wrought special miracles by the hands of Paul (the Apostle): So that from his body were brought unto the sick handkerchiefs or aprons, and the diseases departed from them**, and the evil spirits went out of them.** Then certain of the vagabond Jews, exorcists, took upon them to call over them which had evil spirits the name of the Lord Jesus, saying, We adjure you by Jesus whom Paul preacheth. And there were seven sons of one Sceva, a Jew, and chief of the priests, which did so. **And the evil spirit answered and said, Jesus I know, and Paul I know; but who are ye?** (The Acts of the Apostles 19:11-15).

Bible Christians believed in evil spirits and the evil spirits knew who Jesus Christ was. They knew him from the Pre-Mortal Existence when they rebelled against God and were cast out. They came to earth remembering they supported Satan and they did this in the presence of God their Heavenly Father. They were damned, which means their progression was stopped. They would never be given a body, which means they will never have a resurrected body. They are here to tempt us and persuade us to do evil. Christ had power over them and he gave that power to his apostles.

Do all of the Bible Christians you know believe these scriptures? Mormons believe these scriptures and we believe the "War in Heaven" was between the followers of Jesus Christ and the followers of Satan also called Lucifer a "Son of the Morning." Satan was one of God's children who evidently had a position of authority in our "first estate" because he influenced a great many of the "angels that sinned" to rebel against God their father. Lucifer or Satan, who wanted to "exalt my throne above the stars of God" said "I will be like the most High."

Jesus Christ had been foreordained as the Savior of all mankind (1 Peter 1:19-20). Jesus Christ volunteered to be the Redeemer. He was obedient to His Father and always wanted to do the will of the Father. "For it pleased the Father that in him (Christ) should all fullness dwell" (Colossians 1:19). Jesus Christ was the "firstborn of every creature," "whom He (God) hath appointed heir of all things" (Colossians 1:15 and Hebrews 1:2).

There was open rebellion in heaven in the presence of God. Lucifer, the "father of lies," was cast down with those who followed after him. They **knew** what they were doing; this wasn't a question of belief, it was sure knowledge. Jesus Christ was prepared to atone for the sins of the world before the "foundation of the world." (There was a Savior in place before mortals were on the earth.) The stage was set for the Second Estate of our Heavenly Father's children. We should take comfort in knowing we were not cast down with Satan and his followers. We were obedient and followed Jesus Christ in doing the will of our Father in Heaven. We were anxious to come to earth and receive a mortal body. We understood our earth life was where we could prove ourselves in Heavenly Father's plan of eternal progression. We would not remember our pre-mortal life when we came to earth. Any knowledge of our pre-mortal life would be suspended while we were out of the presence of God.

It has been interesting, as I have had gospel discussions with others, to see them change when they realize that God is actually their Father in Heaven. He is literally the Father of our Spirits. Their prayers are different because they now know their relationship with God. Their relationship with everyone changed when they discovered they were brothers and sisters.

As you read each of the following chapters, I hope what you learn will become a new reality because you realize you are a child of God and that He loves you.

CHAPTER THREE

THE CREATION AND THE FALL

*I*n chapter two, we learned that under the direction of his Father, Jesus Christ created this earth (Heb.1:1-3). We also learned that Jesus Christ was "foreordained before the foundation of the world," which means a Savior and Redeemer was "in place" before the earth was organized and before the "creation of man."

When the earth was ready, "God said, Let **us** make man in **our** image, after **our** likeness… So God created man in his own image, in the image of God created he him; male and female created he them" (Genesis 1:26-27). The first man was Adam and his wife was Eve. God placed them in the Garden of Eden. "And God blessed them, and God said unto them, **Be fruitful, and multiply, and replenish the earth**, and subdue it…"(Genesis 1:28). In other words, God was commanding Adam and Eve, as the first parents, to open the way for all of His spirit children to come to the earth, which is their Second Estate.

Then God gave Adam and Eve another (lesser) commandment, "But of the tree of the knowledge of good and evil, thou shalt not eat of it: for in the day that thou eatest thereof thou shalt surely die" (Genesis 2:17). Adam and Eve were in a state of innocence, they had no knowledge of good and evil. In this condition, they could not keep the first and great commandment, to "be fruitful and multiply." They could not have mortal children, because they were not yet mortal.

To become mortal they needed to eat of the fruit of the tree of knowledge of good and evil. They didn't know that yet, but Satan did and he deceived Eve. He told her she wouldn't die if she ate the fruit of the tree of knowledge of good and evil. He enticed her with "For God doth know that in the day ye eat thereof, then your eyes shall be opened, and ye shall be as gods, knowing good and evil." (Genesis 3:5). Adam and Eve were in a state of innocence, but they still had their "agency" (they had choices). They could choose to remain in the Garden of Eden and have no joy, no sorrow and no children or they could leave the comforts of the Garden of Eden and become mortal and have children as God had commanded them.

Some Bible Christians believe Adam's transgression in the Garden of Eden (eating the fruit of the tree of knowledge of good and evil) was the "Original Sin." They believe Adam's posterity inherited this sin at birth. "Original Sin is the hereditary stain with which we are born on account of our origin or descent from Adam" (Catholic Encyclopedia, vol. 11 pp312-315). "Infant baptism, therefore is a necessary corollary to the doctrine of original sin, since those who die in original sin are deprived of the happiness of heaven" (Catholic Encyclopedia, vol. 2 pp258-274).

You may want to contemplate this scripture, "**And the LORD God said, Behold, the man is become as one of us, to know good and evil...**" (Genesis 3:22). After eating of the fruit of the tree of knowledge of good and evil, Adam and Eve gained something God has. God is good. He is perfect, and He has knowledge of good and evil. God has an awareness of good and evil and chooses to be good. Therefore Adam and Eve's decision to eat of this fruit appears to be a "step up" because they now have a knowledge of good and evil like God and Christ.

I want to share a thoughtful and interesting quote from Time Magazine, May 31, 1954:

> Scientists, once so sure that they were leading mankind out of religious darkness, do not stress the point these days, and churchmen are speaking out quite boldly again about such old-fashioned concepts as Original Sin and The Last Judgment. Last week a prominent scientist did his best to answer back.

> Before the Royal Society of New Zealand's Eighth Science Congress, Australia's top atomic physicist, Marcus Laurence Oliphant, attacked recent statements by Pope Pius XII and Labor Leader Clement R. Atlee citing the misuse of science as a menace to the world. Scientist Oliphant implied that the world's sorry state is the fault of the churches for not doing their job better. 'I can find no evidence whatever,' he said, 'that the

morality of mankind has improved over the 5,000 years or so of recorded history.'

In the Garden of Eden incident, moreover, Prof. Oliphant gladly ranged himself on the side of the Serpent. 'We are told that ...Adam and Eve were driven from the Garden of Eden because they disobeyed the law and ate of the fruit of the tree of knowledge. It seems strange to me that the exercise of the greatest faculty with which man has been endowed should ever have been regarded as a sin... By a deliberate act, probably the greatest step he ever took, (Man) chose to seek knowledge, thereby setting himself apart from all living things and insuring his ultimate dominion over the earth. **What is called the Fall of Man should be known as the Ascent of Man.'**

No wonder there is a conflict between science and religion. Doctrines, like "original sin," have been substituted for recorded doctrines in the Bible. Prof. Oliphant reminds us that Adam and Eve exercised "the greatest faculty with which man had been endowed"– agency or freedom of choice. They chose to have a knowledge of good and evil, which opened the way to mortality. Therefore they had fallen (entered into) the second stage (second estate) of God's plan for man's eternal progression, which prepared them to return to God (or ascend to God). Perhaps we should call the "Fall of Man" the "Ascent of Man." (I don't believe it was Professor Oliphant's intent to teach or clarify this doctrine of the Bible. He did seem to delight in reminding theologians of scriptures that have been forgotten.)

I believe that I need to comment on Satan's role in the Garden of Eden. Satan wanted Adam and Eve to "fall" and become mortal. He wanted them along with their children to fail their test in mortality. He wants them to follow him as the other "evil spirits" have done.

Adam and Eve chose to eat of the fruit of the tree of knowledge of good and evil. The fruit caused their bodies to become mortal. They could now keep the first and most important commandment to "be fruitful and multiply." By this decision the way was provided for the rest of God's spirit children to come to this earth and continue their eternal progression. It is true they broke a commandment (law) and became mortal and would therefore die, but remember Christ had already been foreordained to redeem us from death. The "Fall of Adam" was anticipated by God and Christ. It is difficult to understand why Adam and Eve had to "fall" until you discuss "The Atonement of Jesus Christ." In other words, Earth Life, with a knowledge of good and evil, was always a part of God's Plan of Salvation. Adam's transgression actually brought life, not death, into man's eternal existence. Many of the concerns people have about the role of Adam and Eve as our first parents are better appreciated when we understand the Atonement of Jesus Christ and how it overcomes the effects of "The Fall."

Mormons do not believe in the doctrine of "Original Sin." "We believe that men will be punished for their own sins, and not for Adam's transgression." (Second Article of Faith of The Church of Jesus Christ of Latter-day Saints.) We also believe that the Atonement of Jesus Christ took care of Adam's transgression. "...And the Lord said unto Adam: **Behold I have forgiven thee thy transgression in the Garden of Eden.** Hence came the saying abroad among the people, that **the Son of God hath atoned for original guilt, wherein the sins of the parents cannot be answered upon the heads of the children, for they are whole from the foundation of the world"** (Moses 6:53-54).

When you think about "the Fall of Adam and Eve," remember that because Adam and Eve ate of the tree of knowledge of good and evil:

> They gained a knowledge that God has. "Behold, the man is become as one of us, to know good and evil." Each of us has inherited this attribute of God.

> They became mortal, that meant they could have mortal children, thus fulfilling the first and great commandment of God: "To multiply and replenish the earth."

> They opened the "door" for all of us to come to the earth and continue to progress by proving ourselves here.

> They provided an opportunity for all of us to become resurrected beings like Jesus Christ. We will all receive a resurrected body, which is perfect and will never die.

I could add to this list, but as you read the following chapters, you can make your own list. Please remember if we do not understand "the Fall of Adam and Eve," we will not fully understand the Atonement of Jesus Christ.

The Fall of Adam and Eve brought about a "Physical Death" and a "Spiritual Death" for all of their descendants. When they became mortal they could have mortal children. Our mortal bodies are temporary houses for our spirits. Mortal bodies all die when our spirits separate from them. This separation is called "Physical Death."

When Adam and Eve were cast out of the Garden of Eden, they also were separated from the presence of God. When they had children, they provided mortal bodies for the spirit children of God. At birth these children were also separated from their Heavenly Father. This separation is called "Spiritual Death."

As each of us comes to this earth we are separated from God and experience "Spiritual Death." Because we are mortal, we will eventually experience "Physical Death" and be separated from our mortal bodies. We are all in need of a way to overcome these two deaths. We need a Savior and a Redeemer.

CHAPTER FOUR

THE ATONEMENT OF JESUS CHRIST

*T*his chapter has been the most difficult one to write. My concern is for you as the reader. How do I say all that needs to be said about Jesus Christ? How do I convey to each of you how important Christ can be in your life? The Atonement of Jesus Christ is the fundamental doctrine of all scripture. Therefore this chapter may be the most important chapter in the book. Without Christ there is no "Plan of Salvation." Mormons believe this. I hope you believe this.

It seems appropriate to repeat these scriptures:

For God so loved the world, that He gave his only begotten Son, that whosoever believeth in him should not perish, but have everlasting life (John 3:16).

But with the precious blood of Christ, as of a lamb without blemish and without spot: Who verily was preordained before the foundation of the world, but was manifest in these last times for you (1 Peter 1:19-20).

Our Heavenly Father and His Son, Jesus Christ, do not want us to "perish." They want us to have everlasting life. They want to save us from "physical death" (the death of the body) and even more importantly from "spiritual death" (separation from God). Through the Atonement of Jesus Christ, this has been provided for all of us. Jesus voluntarily agreed "before the foundation of the world" to take upon himself the sins of the world. We do not comprehend how he accomplished this unbelievable sacrifice, but we can know he did.

The word "Atonement" can be better understood by dividing the word into three words: at-one-ment. It means reconciliation, the bringing into agreement those who have been separated.

After Jesus had shared the Last Supper with his apostles he went to the Garden of Gethsemane to pray and prepare for his atonement for all of us:

> Saying, Father, if thou be willing, remove this cup from me: nevertheless not my will, but thine, be done. And there appeared an angel unto him from heaven, strengthening him. **And being in an agony he prayed more earnestly: and his sweat was as it were great drops of blood falling down to the ground** (Luke 22:42-44).

Can you imagine the pain he must have suffered which caused "great drops of blood" to leave his body as sweat from every pore? There were no persecutors there at this time, not in the Garden of Gethsemane. His hour had come. He was in agony, both body and spirit. This is what he came to earth to do for all of God's children. His Father sent an angel from heaven to strengthen him before his sacrifice.

Jesus Christ took upon himself the sins and sorrows of all of us. For this reason he came to earth, born of an earthly mother (Mary) and of an immortal Father. Because of his mortal mother, Jesus had the capacity to die. Because of his immortal Father he had the ability to withstand death. He could determine the time he would die and complete the atonement. His life could not be taken until he was ready to give it:

> **Therefore doth my Father love me, because I lay down my life, that I might take it again. No man taketh it from me, but I lay it down of myself. I have power to lay it down, and I have power to take it again. This commandment have I received of my Father** (John 10:17-18).

Another attribute of Jesus Christ was his perfect life which made it possible for him to vicariously assume our sins. He was without sin. He was the "lamb without blemish and without spot" (1 Peter 1:19). "Though he were a Son, yet learned he obedience by the things which he suffered; **And being made perfect, he became the author of eternal salvation unto all them that obey him;**" (Hebrews 5:8-9).

Jesus Christ was foreordained in Heaven to come to this earth and become our Savior and our Redeemer. He knew his place and his part in the Plan of Salvation of mankind. Jesus said: "I am the way, the truth, and the life: no man cometh unto the Father, but by me" (John 14:6).

Jesus Christ overcame "physical death" personally and for all mankind through his literal resurrection. His spirit after three days in the Spirit World returned to the body that lay in the tomb. He rose from the **dead never to die again**. Because of his atonement and resurrection, all of Adam's posterity will be resurrected:

> Now if Christ be preached that he rose from the dead, how say some among you that there is no resurrection of the dead?... **If in this life only we have hope in Christ, we are of all men most miserable. But now is Christ risen from the dead, and become the first fruits of them that slept**. For since by man came death, by man came also the resurrection of the dead. **For as in Adam all die, even so in Christ shall all be made alive. But every man in his own order: Christ the first fruits; afterward they that are Christ's at his coming** (1 Corinthians 15:12, 19-23).

Our resurrection is assured through the Atonement of Jesus Christ. We only need to be concerned about when we will be resurrected and to what we will be resurrected.

Jesus Christ has also opened the way for us to overcome "spiritual death" however, it is conditional. Remember "spiritual death" is being separated from Heavenly Father. "Know ye not that the unrighteous shall not inherit the kingdom of God?" (1 Corinthians 6:9).

Because of his perfect atonement, Jesus Christ became the author of our salvation. "Though he were a Son, yet learned he obedience by the things which he suffered; **And being made perfect, he became the author of eternal salvation unto all them that obey him** " (Hebrews 5:8-9).

We not only must **believe** in Jesus Christ we must **understand** his gospel (teachings) and **follow** them. The Apostle Paul said: "**For I am not ashamed of the gospel of Christ: for it is the power of God unto salvation to every one that believeth;...** " (Romans 1:16).

I have quoted scriptures from the Bible about what Jesus Christ has done for us. Next we will see what the Bible tells us we must do to accept Christ and his atonement.

CHAPTER FIVE

FAITH IN THE LORD JESUS CHRIST

*J*esus said: **"I am the way, the truth, and the life: no man cometh unto the Father, but by me"** (John 14:6). If we want to return to our Father in Heaven we need to accept Jesus Christ, our Savior, who is the way back. Jesus also said: **"If a man love me, he will keep my words: and my Father will love him, and we will come unto him, and make our abode with him"** (John 14:23). This is not an empty promise. You are not alone in your search for the truth. Christ has promised you an assurance that will sustain you. **"Peace I leave with you, my peace I give unto you: not as the world giveth, give I unto you. Let not your heart be troubled, neither let it be afraid"** (John 14:27).

If we want this peace then our quest has begun. It starts with a desire, a hope for something better than we have at the present time. If we are sincere in our hope that Jesus Christ will show us the way then we are on the path. **"But without faith it is impossible to please him: for he that cometh to God must believe that he is,** and that he is a rewarder of them that diligently seek him" (Hebrews 11:6).

Do we have faith in Christ or do we just believe in Christ? The words faith and believe are often used interchangeably in the Bible, but their meanings are different today. We speak of belief as an intellectual assent, which is usually passive, whereas the word faith implies a more sure conviction that is acted upon. So do we just believe in Christ or do we have a committed faith to follow Christ?

Perhaps the Apostle Paul's explanation will help us understand the meaning of faith. **"Now faith is the substance (assurance) of things hoped for, the evidence of things not seen"** (Hebrews

11:1). Faith is an ongoing process substantiated with evidence. Jesus said: "My doctrine is not mine, but his that sent me. If any man will do his will, he shall know of the doctrine, whether it be of God, or whether I speak of myself" (John 7:16-17). Christ said to his disciples: **"If ye continue in my word, then are ye my disciples in deed; And ye shall know the truth, and the truth shall make you free"** (John 8:31-32). We can know the truth by "continuing in his word," which is the faith process. We can know Jesus Christ is our savior and the way back to the Father. When we know that we will be free of ignorance, doubt, insecurity, hopelessness and sin. We will have the peace that Jesus promised us.

Our faith in Jesus Christ must extend to a faith in our Father in Heaven and in the Holy Ghost. We can gain that faith through our individual prayers to our Heavenly Father. We receive answers to our prayers through the Holy Ghost. Jesus taught: "But the Comforter, which is the Holy Ghost, whom the Father will send in my name, he shall teach you all things, and bring all things to your remembrance, whatsoever I have said unto you" (John 14:26).

The Holy Ghost is the third member of the Godhead. He is a special messenger from God and Christ. Jesus taught this to his apostles: **"But when the Comforter is come, whom I will send unto you from the Father, even the Spirit of truth, which proceedeth from the Father, he shall testify of me"** (John 15:26).

We can know who God and Christ are because the Holy Ghost will testify of them to those who diligently seek. We need to remember these words of Christ: **"And this is life eternal, that they might know thee the only true God, and Jesus Christ, whom thou hast sent"** (John 17:3).

Here is a real-life illustration of how the "faith process" works. In 1960 I met Kirk, a young man who was a senior at the University of Washington. We were discussing life insurance when he told me he had met Paula, an attractive airline stewardess who was a Mormon and he thought they would get married. He went into the Army and married this young lady. After leaving the Army they moved to Seattle. I called him and found out he was not going to any church. He was a "passive Christian" at the time.

He agreed to meet with me and we discussed "Bible Christianity" over a period of six months. He listened attentively and believed me intellectually. He thought it was all reasonable, but did nothing about it except meet with me and listen. I asked him why he wasn't putting the gospel of Jesus Christ first in his life, because that was what his family needed. After this admonition he began to find time to study the scriptures, to pray sincerely for answers, to attend church and to live the way Christ asked him to live. These are the elements of the "faith process." In doing those things, he was complying with this invitation from the Savior:

> **Ask, and it shall be given you; seek, and ye shall find; knock, and it shall be opened unto you: For everyone that asketh receiveth; he that seeketh findeth; and to him that knocketh it shall be opened** (Matthew 7:7-8).

He told me that one day he was prayerfully reading the Gospel of Matthew and suddenly knew that Jesus Christ really lived, and everything fell into place. The gospel of Jesus Christ was the way back to Heavenly Father. He understood what he was reading and it became not only interesting but very important to him. He was converted to the gospel of Jesus Christ and would never be the same again. Forty years later he wrote me a letter and said "The greatest gift of my life, one that cannot be exceeded in mortality, was that of the Holy Ghost witnessing to me that the fullness of the gospel of Jesus Christ was on the earth and I was to be baptized."

Kirk's life was changed because he did something about his belief in Christ. His faith led to conversion and Kirk and Paula raised a righteous posterity of believing Christians. His life is a confirmation of what the Apostle James taught:

> **What doth it profit, my brethren, though a man say he hath faith, and have not works? Can faith save him? ...Even so faith, if it hath not works, is dead, being alone. Yea, a man may say, Thou hast faith, and I have works: shew me thy faith without thy works, and I will shew thee my faith by my works.** ...Seest thou how faith wrought with his works, and by works was faith made perfect? ...Ye see then how that by works a man is justified, and not by faith only. ...**For as the body without the spirit is dead, so faith without works is dead also** (James 2:14, 17-18, 22, 24, 26).

Mormons, who do good works because of their faith in Jesus Christ are following the admonition of James. Jesus said: "If ye love me, keep my commandments" (John 14:15). Can we keep his commandments without "good works"? I suppose we could always question the motive of a fellow Christian's good works, but why would we? Are we their judges?

As we apply the atonement of Christ in our lives, we should not confuse "Faith" and "Grace." Grace does not require works, but it does require faith. "For by grace are you saved through faith: and that not of yourselves: it is the gift of God: Not of works, lest any man should boast" (Ephesians 2:8-9).

We have already defined what faith is, now we will talk about "grace." I believe the Apostle Paul explained it well to the Corinthian saints of the Church of Jesus Christ. Paul had a weakness which he asked the Lord to remove. The Lord answered his prayer: **"And he said unto me, My grace is sufficient for thee: for my strength is made perfect in weakness"** (2 Corinthians 12:1-12, v9). Paul already had faith in God, that's why he asked him to remove the weakness. He got a different answer than he was expecting. The Lord told him his weakness was a reminder to stay humble and then he would receive God's help (God's strength). Paul learned that, when faced with adversity, even persecution, he needed to turn to the Lord for his grace. His grace is a divine power that Paul called "the power of Christ" and "God's strength." In essence Paul was told his weakness kept him humble and his humility opened the door to God's grace or strength. He simply said: "...for when I am weak (humble), then am I strong" (I have God's strength) (v 10).

If this explanation of grace is new to you, consider the words of another apostle: "But he giveth more grace. Wherefore he saith, God resisteth the proud, **but giveth grace unto the humble**" (James 4:6). And again: **"Humble yourselves in the sight of the Lord, and he shall lift you up"** (James 4:10).

By faith we can **know** "the strength of God" and "the power of Christ." By grace we magnify our faith and we **receive** the "strength of God" and "the power of Christ."

CHAPTER SIX

OUR FAITH GROWS WITH REPENTANCE

$\mathcal{M}$ormons are often accused of "working their way to Heaven." When did "working" get such a bad name? We read in scripture, "For the Son of man shall come in the glory of his Father with his angels; **and then he shall reward every man according to his works**" (Matthew 16:27). The Apostle James said:

> Even so faith, if it hath not works, is dead, being alone. Yea, a man may say, Thou hast faith, and I have works; shew me thy faith without thy works, and I will shew thee my faith by my works. Thou believest that there is one God; thou doest well: the devils also believe, and tremble. **But wilt thou know, O vain man, that faith without works is dead?"** Then James illustrated the Prophet Abraham's faith by his works and said: **"...Seest thou how faith wrought with his works, and by works was faith made perfect?** (James 2:17-20, 22).

Some Christians who do "good works" hope they will make up for their lack of faith. I believe this is what the Apostle Matthew was talking about when he quoted the Savior, who said:

> **Not every one that saith unto me, Lord, Lord, shall enter into the kingdom of heaven; but he that doeth the will of my Father which is in heaven.** Many will say to me in that day, Lord, Lord, have we not prophesied in thy name? and in thy name have cast out devils? **and in thy name done many wonderful works?**

And then will I profess unto them, I never knew you: depart from me, ye that work iniquity (Matthew 7:21-23).

We should be careful not to criticize the "good works" of those who have a sincere faith in Christ and his gospel. What are the good works that should proceed from our faith in Christ?

The Apostle Peter answered this question for those on the Day of Pentecost who now believed in what the apostles had taught them about Jesus Christ:

> Now when they heard this, they were pricked in their heart, and said unto Peter and to the rest of the apostles, Men and brethren, what shall we do? **Then Peter said unto them, Repent, and be baptized every one of you in the name of Jesus Christ for the remission of sins, and ye shall receive the gift of the Holy Ghost.** For the promise is unto you, and to your children, and to all that are afar off, even as many as the Lord our God shall call. ...Then they that gladly received his word were baptized: and the same day there were added unto them about three thousand souls... And the Lord added to the church daily such as should be saved (Acts 2:37-39, 41, 47).

Note that these people believed their faith required them to do something. These "Bible Christians" were taught they must repent of their sins and be baptized for a remission of those sins, and they then would receive the gift of the Holy Ghost by the laying on of hands (Acts 8:17-18). This is the doctrine of Jesus Christ and it has not changed.

What are sins? Who has sinned? How do we repent of our sins?

"Whosoever committeth sin transgresseth also the law: **for sin is the transgression of the law**" (1 John 3:4).

"If we say that we have no sin, we deceive ourselves, and the truth is not in us" (1 John 1:8).

"Therefore to him that knoweth to do good, and doeth it not, to him it is sin" (James 4:17).

"For all have sinned, and come short of the glory of God;" (Romans 3:23).

"Now I rejoice, not that ye were made sorry, but that ye sorrowed to repentance: for ye were made sorry after a godly manner... For godly sorrow worketh repentance to salvation..." *(2 Corinthians 7:9-10).*

When we break the laws of God we commit sin. Godly sorrow means we are sorry for breaking one of God's laws, not just sorry we got caught. When we came to this earth we knew we would make mistakes and fail to keep all of God's commandments. If we have faith in Christ, his atonement covers all the sins of which we repent.

We repent of our sins by expressing sorrow to God and asking His forgiveness, by restoring what we can of that which was lost due to our disobedience, and by altogether turning away from our sins and toward God. Repentance is not just a state of mind, it is an action. It is the work we do to bring us closer to God.

What laws are we expected to obey? The Ten Commandments. They haven't been dismissed. They are not obsolete. They are as essential and true today as they were when the Prophet Moses received them from the Lord.

The Ten Commandments (Exodus 20:1-17)

1. Thou shalt have no other gods before me.

2. Thou shalt not make unto thee any graven image, or any likeness of anything that is in heaven above, or that is in the earth beneath, or that is in the water under the earth: Thou shalt not bow down thyself to them, nor serve them: for I the LORD thy God am a jealous God, visiting the iniquity of the fathers upon the children unto the third and fourth generation of them that hate me; And showing mercy unto thousands of them that love me, and keep my commandments.

3. Thou shalt not take the name of the LORD thy God in vain; for the LORD will not hold him guiltless that taketh his name in vain.

4. Remember the sabbath day, to keep it holy. Six days shalt thou labour, and do all thy work: But the seventh day is the sabbath of the LORD thy God: in it thou shalt not do any work, thou, nor thy son, nor thy daughter, thy

manservant, nor thy maidservant, nor thy cattle, nor thy stranger that is within thy gates: For in six days the LORD made heaven and earth, the sea, and all that in them is, and rested the seventh day: wherefore the LORD blessed the sabbath day, and hallowed it.

5.   Honour thy father and thy mother: that thy days may be long upon the land which the LORD thy God giveth thee.

6.   Thou shalt not kill.

7.   Thou shalt not commit adultery.

8.   Thou shalt not steal.

9.   Thou shalt not bear false witness against thy neighbor.

10.   Thou shalt not covet thy neighbour's house, thou shalt not covet thy neighbour's wife, nor his manservant, nor his maid servant, nor his ox, nor his ass, nor any thing that is thy neighbour's.

The Two Great Commandments:

Jesus said: "Thou shalt love the Lord thy God with all thy heart, and with all thy soul, and with all thy mind. This is the first and great commandment. And the second is like unto it, Thou shalt love thy neighbor as thyself. On these two commandments hang all the law and the prophets" (Matthew 22:37-40).

Christ's Sermon on the Mount (Matthew 5, 6, 7)

The Redeeming Principles and Ordinances of the Gospel of Jesus Christ (Chapters 5, 6 and 7 of this book)

After reviewing all of the above commandments, consider this view of each commandment:

There is a law, irrevocably decreed in Heaven before the foundations of this world, upon which all blessings are predicated–And when we obtain any blessing from God, it is by obedience to that law upon which it is predicated (Doctrine and Covenants 130:20-21).

In other words, God gives us commandments so we can receive the blessings that come from living His laws.

An example of a commandment with a promised blessing is the law of the tithe given to the Israelites (the covenant people of God):

> Even from the days of your fathers ye are gone away from mine ordinances, and have not kept them. Return unto me, and I will return unto you, saith the LORD of hosts. But ye said, Wherein shall we return? Will a man rob God? Yet ye have robbed me. But ye say, Wherein have we robbed thee? **In tithes and offerings.** Ye are cursed with a curse: for ye have robbed me, even this whole nation. **Bring ye all the tithes into the storehouse, that there may be meat in mine house, and prove me now herewith, saith the LORD of hosts, if I will not open you the windows of heaven, and pour you out a blessing, that there shall not be room enough to receive it. And I will rebuke the devourer for your sakes, and he shall not destroy the fruits of your ground; neither shall your vine cast her fruit before the time in the field, saith the LORD of hosts. And all nations shall call you blessed: for you shall be a delightsome land, saith the LORD of hosts** (Malachi 3:7-12).

What a remarkable promise for keeping the Law of Tithing. Tithing is one tenth of our income or increase. If we have faith in this law of the Lord, we will pay tithing and God will bless us. "I, the Lord, am bound when ye do what I say; but when ye do not what I say, ye have no promise" (Doctrine and Covenants 82:10).

In 1992 I insured a new dentist in a group of health professionals. My dentist had retired, so my new client became my dentist. I learned she was going through a divorce and had two young children. Also, her mother died and she was a little overwhelmed. We met off and on for over a year and her problems never went away. She postponed living the commandments. One day I asked her to read this scripture:

> **They were slow to hearken unto the voice of the Lord their God; therefore, the Lord their God is slow to hearken unto their prayers, to answer them in the day of their trouble. In the day of their peace they esteemed lightly my counsel; but, in the day of their trouble, of necessity they feel after me** (Doctrine and Covenants 101:7-8).

I let that sink in and then asked her: "Do you know what the word hearken means?" She quickly responded, "I know what you are getting at." She then broke down and wept. She knew hearken meant more than hearing the word of God. It meant doing something about it. She needed to be obedient to the teachings of Jesus Christ. True faith in Christ and his gospel requires a "broken heart" and true repentance. From that day on she began the "faith with works" process and she started receiving the blessings that come from keeping the commandments. She was baptized on September 4, 1994.

Faith without repentance (works) is dead. If we want the Savior's grace (help) we must live his gospel, we must keep his commandments. If our only motivation for obeying the commandments is to receive the blessings, then we start there. Remember faith is a process and obedience is how we demonstrate our faith in the Savior and his gospel. As we learn to follow the Savior because we love him, then we will take "work" out of keeping his commandments. It will take this kind of faith and commitment to live all of the commandments.

Repentance means we have to change. Change is never easy, but it is necessary. Here is a sobering thought:

> For behold, I, God, have suffered these things for all, that they might not suffer if they would repent; But if they would not repent they must suffer even as I; Which suffering caused myself, even God, the greatest of all, to tremble because of pain, and to bleed at every pore, and to suffer both body and spirit…Doctrine and Covenants, Section 19:16-18).

Jesus Christ is our Savior. He has already atoned for our sins. All he requires from us is to have faith in him and repent of our sins and obey his commandments. Here is his plea to you:

> Come unto me, all ye that labour and are heavy laden, and I will give you rest. Take my yoke upon you, and learn of me; for I am meek and lowly in heart: and ye shall find rest unto your souls. For my yoke is easy, and my burden is light (Matthew 11:28-30).

Procrastination only postpones the blessings we and our family need. The noted American philosopher, William James, said: "If we want to change, we have to change." This is what repentance is all about.

CHAPTER SEVEN

BAPTISM AND THE GIFT OF THE HOLY GHOST

*O*bviously early Christians in the Bible believed in the ordinance of baptism as a requirement to accept Christ and his atonement. Jesus Christ set the example when he was baptized by John the Baptist even though he was without sin. The conversation Jesus had with John at that time helps us understand the importance of baptism:

> Then cometh Jesus from Galilee to Jordan unto John, to be baptized of him. But John forbad him, saying, I have need to be baptized of thee, and comest thou to me? And Jesus answering said unto him, **Suffer (permit) it to be so now: for thus it becometh us to fulfil all righteousness.** Then he suffered (permitted) him (Matthew 3:13-15).

If Jesus who was without any sin needed to be baptized to "fulfil all righteousness," then all of God's children **who are accountable** need to be baptized in like manner.

All four gospels in the New Testament record the baptism of Jesus Christ by John the Baptist. How was Jesus baptized?

> **And Jesus, when he was baptized, went up straightway out of the water**: and, lo, the heavens were opened unto him, and he saw the Spirit of God descending like a dove, and lighting upon him: And lo a voice from heaven, saying, This is my beloved Son, in whom I am well pleased (Matthew 3:16-17).

Jesus didn't go into the river Jordan to be sprinkled. He was immersed in the river and **"came straightway out of the water."** Jesus was baptized by John who had the authority (priesthood) to baptize him.

The baptism of Jesus Christ was such an essential ordinance and example for us, that all members of the Godhead (Father, Son and Holy Ghost) were present. The Holy Ghost was there evidenced by the appearance of a dove, which is a sign of the Holy Ghost. Our Father in Heaven spoke from Heaven saying, "This is my beloved Son, in whom I am well pleased" (Matthew 3:17). All four gospels record the same experience.

Each of us should follow the example of our Savior, because our baptism is a witness to him and our Father in Heaven that we too want to **"fulfil all righteousness"** and accept his atonement. Our Father in Heaven will also be pleased when we are baptized.

In 1997 I was asked by my dentist to baptize her son, who had turned age eight (the age of accountability). At the baptism I met her friend, Scott, who had been invited to the baptismal service. Shortly after the baptism, he and I began meeting, because he was interested in marrying my dentist and she wanted him to accept what she believed before talking about marriage. He was raised Catholic, but at the time was opposed to any "organized religion." Our meetings were intense and Scott was a great student. He requested baptism and on June 26, 1997 he was baptized. Before going down into the baptismal font, Scott asked if we could have a personal prayer. I knew he was ready to enter into a covenant with the Lord.

Baptism is a personal covenant we make with the Lord promising we will follow him and keep his commandments. Through baptism we are promised a "remission of our sins" if we have truly repented of them before baptism. Baptism is the way we enter the "kingdom of God" on earth, which is the Church of Jesus Christ.

Jesus told Nicodemus, a ruler of the Jews:

Verily, verily, I say unto thee, Except a man be born of water and of the Spirit, he cannot enter into the kingdom of God (John 3:5).

Baptism into Christ's church precedes the ordinance of laying on of hands to receive "the gift of the Holy Ghost."

The baptismal covenant is renewed each Sunday when members of the Church of Jesus Christ take the sacrament in remembrance of Christ's atonement:

> And they continued stedfastly in the apostles' doctrine and fellowship**, and in breaking of bread, and in prayers"** (Acts 2:42).

On the day of Pentecost, the Apostle Peter and the other apostles were blessed with the extraordinary gift of "speaking in tongues," which is one of the gifts of the Holy Ghost:

> And they were all filled with the Holy Ghost, and began to speak with other tongues, as the Spirit gave them utterance. And there were dwelling at Jerusalem Jews, devout men, out of every nation under heaven. Now when this was noised abroad, the multitude came together, and were confounded**, because that every man heard them speak in his own language. …we do hear them speak in our tongues the wonderful works of God** (Acts 2:4-6, 11).

> But Peter, standing up with the eleven (apostles), lifted up his voice, and said unto them, Ye men of Judea, and all ye that dwell at Jerusalem, be this known unto you, and hearken to my words: For these are not drunken, as ye suppose, seeing it is but the third hour of the day (Acts 2:14-15).

The people thought the apostles were drunk because they were able to speak different languages than their own. This ability is called "the gift of tongues" and the purpose of this gift is to preach the gospel of Christ in different languages. Peter continues:

> This Jesus hath God raised up, whereof we all are witnesses. Therefore being by the right hand of God exalted, and having received of the Father the promise of the Holy Ghost, he hath shed forth this, which ye now see and hear (Acts 2:32-33).

> Now when they heard this, they were pricked in their heart, and said unto Peter and to the rest of the apostles, Men and brethren, what shall we do? Then Peter said unto them**, Repent, and be**

baptized every one of you in the name of Jesus Christ for the remission of sins, and ye shall receive the gift of the Holy Ghost. For the promise is unto you, and to your children, and to all that are afar off, even as many as the Lord our God shall call. And with many other words did he testify and exhort, saying, Save yourselves from this untoward (crooked) generation. Then they that gladly received his word were baptized: and the same day there were added unto them about three thousand souls (Acts 2:37-41).

The Holy Ghost is the third member of the Godhead. He is a personage of Spirit. He is a messenger from Christ and our Father in Heaven. When Christ was preparing his apostles for his death, he promised to send the Holy Ghost after he ascended back to Heaven:

But the Comforter, which is the Holy Ghost, whom the Father will send in my name, he shall teach you all things, and bring all things to your remembrance, whatsoever I have said unto you (John 14:26).

Christ told his apostles:

I have yet many things to say unto you, but ye cannot bear them now. Howbeit when he, the Spirit of truth (the Holy Ghost), is come, he will guide you into all truth: for he shall not speak of himself; but whatsoever he shall hear, that shall he speak; and he will shew you things to come. He shall glorify me: for he shall receive of mine, and shall shew it unto you (John 16:12-14).

The Apostles received revelations from Christ and Heavenly Father through the Holy Ghost. They gained their faith (testimony) that Jesus Christ was the Son of God and the Savior by revelation through the Holy Ghost. "But when the Comforter is come, whom I will send unto you from the Father, even the Spirit of truth, which proceedeth from the Father, **he shall testify of me:** And ye also shall bear witness, because ye have been with me from the beginning" (John 15:26-27).

Remember **faith is a process**. It is the way we can know the truth. We can know Jesus Christ is our Savior and that the gospel of Jesus Christ (his teachings and commandments) is necessary to return to our Father in Heaven. The Apostle Paul said: **"For I am not** ashamed of the gospel of Christ: for it is the power of God unto salvation to every one that believeth; to the Jews first, and also to the Greek" (Romans 1:16). We can know, even like the early Bible Christians knew, because the Holy Ghost "will teach you all things" (John 14:26). We need to study the scriptures, obey the commandments, and pray to our Father in Heaven in the name of Jesus Christ for our own testimony. The Holy Ghost will testify (witness) that Jesus Christ is our Savior. The Holy Ghost will guide us as we grow in faith and repent of our sins and prepare for baptism.

After baptism we are given the "gift of the Holy Ghost" by the "laying on of hands" by those who have the authority:

> **Then laid they (the apostles) their hands on them, and they received the Holy Ghost. And when Simon saw that through laying on of the apostles' hands the Holy Ghost was given,** he offered them money, Saying, Give me also this power, that on whomsoever I lay hands, he may receive the Holy Ghost. But Peter said unto him, Thy money perish with thee, because thou hast thought that the gift of God may be purchased with money (Acts 8:17-20).

The "gift of the Holy Ghost" means that we have the Holy Ghost as our constant companion as long as we remain faithful. It also means we have access to some of the "gifts of the spirit" which the Apostle Paul talks about to the church members in Corinth:

> Now concerning spiritual gifts, brethren, I would not have you ignorant. ...But the manifestation of the Spirit is given to every man to profit withal. For to one is given by the Spirit the word of wisdom; to another the word of knowledge by the same Spirit; To another faith by the same Spirit; to another the gifts of healing by the same Spirit; To another the working of miracles; to another prophecy; to another discerning of spirits; to another divers kinds of tongues; to another the interpretation of tongues: But all these worketh that one and the selfsame Spirit, dividing to every man severally as he will (1 Corinthians 12:1, 7-11).

The early Bible Christians believed in the first principles and ordinances of the gospel of Jesus Christ which are: faith, repentance, baptism and the gift of the Holy Ghost by the laying on of hands.

CHAPTER EIGHT

THE GOSPEL OF CHRIST IS PREACHED TO THOSE WHO HAVE DIED

*I*n 1994 my wife, Norma, and I accepted a call to serve a mission for The Church of Jesus Christ of Latter-day Saints in Independence, Missouri. We invited friends and neighbors, including some agents and their wives to an "Open House" at our home. Surprisingly the ex-wife of a former agent came. Keiko (Kay) has an interesting background. She was born in Japan, the child of a Japanese woman and a U. S. serviceman stationed in Japan after World War II. Her father had hoped to bring Kay and her mother to America, but that was discouraged then. She had a very difficult childhood.

Her mother became a Christian and prayed for the non-denominational missionary couple to adopt her daughter. They did so and they brought her to America. She knew her Bible well, but she had been on a long spiritual search for the church that was described in the New Testament. She said, "I needed a 'home church.' So for nine years, I searched for the right church. I visited most of the Protestant churches, Catholic churches, Jewish Christian churches, Buddhist and explored the teachings of Islam. I had an open mind, but knew in my heart this church must be Christ-centered. This is what the Bible taught. I had learned it as a young girl by my adoptive American parents and had accepted the Bible (both the Old and New Testament) as the inspired word of God. The Protestant church where we attended as a family didn't fulfill all of my questions. I started on a search for the 'right church.'" Her long search ended when she was baptized on November 21, 1998 into The Church of Jesus Christ of Latter-day Saints.

Her story is here because what I have written in the seven previous chapters is what I taught her. She was already a believing Bible Christian, but she was amazed at the new things she learned from the Bible as we talked. One pleasant surprise was the answer to what happens to those who didn't believe in Jesus Christ when they died. Her Japanese ancestors needed salvation too, but no one taught her how they could be saved. So we will now revisit the first chapter and talk some more about "Life After Death."

You may remember in the first chapter, we talked about the "Spirit World" as a place where our spirits go after we die. What happens in the "Spirit World?" Why is it important for us to know who our ancestors are? This is a most important question if our ancestors were not Christians. I am going to repeat a scripture which is most comforting and necessary for this discussion. **"For for this cause was the gospel preached also to them that are dead, that they might be judged according to men in the flesh, but live according to God in the spirit"** (1 Peter 4:6). I quoted this to a retired Protestant minister recently and after thinking about it he asked me where it was in the Bible.

This may be one of the most overlooked scriptures in the Bible and it helps answer a question for which almost all of today's Christians have no answer. So let's make sure we understand it. The word gospel means "good news." The good news is—Jesus Christ has made a perfect atonement for all mankind. We commonly use the word gospel in place of "the teachings of Jesus Christ," which must be lived so we can return to God and be saved. An example of this is in Romans 1:16. The Apostle Paul said: "For I am not ashamed of the gospel of Christ: for it is the power of God unto salvation to everyone that believeth..."

Therefore when the gospel of Christ is preached to those who have died, it is the power of God unto their salvation if they believe it. **This means in the Spirit World these teachings of Jesus Christ are being taught: Faith in Jesus Christ and his atonement, repentance of sins, baptism for a remission of sins, and the gift of the Holy Ghost.** The gospel of Jesus Christ doesn't change after we die, we will just understand it better and have a greater faith. Our spirit retains the knowledge and experiences we have learned here on earth during mortality. Therefore those who have gained a testimony of

Jesus Christ will continue to teach his gospel after they die. They may even have the privilege to teach their ancestors.

Christ opened the way for the gospel to be preached to those who have died. **"For Christ also hath once suffered for sins, the just for the unjust, that he might bring us to God, being put to death in the flesh, but quickened by the Spirit: By which also he went and preached unto the spirits in prison…" (the spirit world)** (1 Peter 3:18-19). The Church of Jesus Christ is also in the spirit world. Those who have died are still free to choose; they have agency just like they had here on earth.

You may now be saying to yourself, "Then why should I worry? I am going to have another chance after I die so I might as well wait and see." Do you believe a procrastinator in this life is not going to be a procrastinator in the spirit world? In my opinion the same spirit that inhabits this earthly body is the same spirit that goes to the spirit world. Why would we change there if we didn't change (repent) here? At least in this life we have "death" as a constant reminder that this part of our life is coming to an end. For this reason we occasionally hear about "death-bed repentance." The Spirit World is more of a "second place" to hear the gospel than a "second chance" to hear the gospel. Those who have had an opportunity in this life should not feel complacent about getting another chance. Consider this: after we die there is no death of the spirit. If there is no death of the spirit, why would we want to change? It will appear that life in the spirit world is going to go on forever. The only way we leave the spirit world is by resurrection. However, even most of the righteous spirits will not be resurrected until the Second Coming of Jesus Christ, and no man knows when that will be. So life in the spirit world will appear to be endless except for those who have accepted the gospel of Christ and are awaiting their resurrection.

What can we do in the Spirit World to accept the atonement of Jesus Christ and what can't we do there? In the Spirit World we can gain a testimony of Jesus Christ as our Savior, and have faith in him. We can learn his teachings and commandments and repent of our sins. The next requirement is baptism for a remission of our sins. However, baptism is an earthly ordinance. How do spirits comply with this commandment?

Before I give you an answer, let us confirm that baptism is essential. Let's review the scriptures about baptism. Christ was baptized to "fulfil all righteousness" and he was without sin (Matthew 3:15). Can we be excused? Christ told his apostles: "Go ye therefore, and teach all nations, baptizing them in the name of the Father, and of the Son, and of the Holy Ghost" (Matthew 28:19). "He that believeth and is baptized shall be saved" (Mark 16:16). The Apostle Peter taught, "Repent, and be baptized every one of you in the name of Jesus Christ for the remission of sins..." (Acts 2:38).

Baptism is an essential ordinance to be saved, even for those who have died without being baptized. The answer is in a letter of the Apostle Paul to the saints at Corinth. Paul is writing about resurrection and he is chiding some of the Jews (the Sadducees who don't believe in a literal resurrection). **"Else what shall they do which are baptized for the dead, if the dead rise not at all? why are they then baptized for the dead?"** (1 Corinthians 15:29).

The early Bible Christians performed baptisms for those who had died. A living person acted as a proxy and was baptized for a deceased person, which is a vicarious act in behalf of those who could not do it for themselves. If this seems strange, then consider that Jesus Christ's atonement was a vicarious act for all of us. He took upon himself our sins, which we could not do for ourselves.

I need to make one thing clear about baptisms for those who have died. This does not mean those people have accepted the baptism. We know they will be taught the gospel of Jesus Christ in the Spirit World, but we don't know whether they will accept it. We hope they will and therefore we do genealogical research in order to find our ancestors and do baptisms for them.

What about baptism for children who have died? The Catholic Church has long taught that children who died in infancy did not go to heaven, but they go to Limbo.

> "After several years of study, the Vatican's International Theological Commission said there are good reasons to hope that babies who die without being baptized go to heaven." In a 41 page document published April 20, 2007, titled "The Hope of Salvation for Infants Who Die Without Being Baptized"... "the commission said the traditional concept of limbo—as a place where unbaptized infants spend eternity but without communion with God—seemed to reflect an 'unduly restrictive view of salvation.'"

"The document traced the development of church thinking about the fate of unbaptized children, noting that there is 'no explicit answer' from Scripture or tradition. ...The church continues to teach that, because of original sin, baptism is the ordinary way of salvation for all people and urges parents to baptize infants, the document said. ...Limbo has never been defined as church dogma and is not mentioned in the current Catechism of the Catholic Church, which states simply that unbaptized infants are entrusted to God's mercy.

"...It must be clearly acknowledged that the church does not have sure knowledge about the salvation of unbaptized infants who die.

"Through the centuries, popes and church councils were careful not to define limbo as a doctrine of the faith and to leave the question open. That was important in allowing an evolution of the teaching, the theological commission said. ...The 30-member International Theological Commission acts as an advisory panel to the Vatican, in particular to the Congregation for the Doctrine of the Faith. Its documents are not considered expressions of authoritative church teaching, but they sometimes set the stage for official Vatican pronouncements."

The reason I have included these last three paragraphs is to show that after 2,000 years the Catholic Church is still troubled about what happens to unbaptized children who have died. They would like to find a way to get them into Heaven, but they don't know how. This is an indication of the possibility that there may be some doctrine that is incorrect (such as "original sin") or that some things are missing from the Bible. I am now going to make an exception again from teaching everything from the Bible and share with you a scripture which contains the simple answer to this question that has troubled great minds in the Catholic Church:

Listen to the words of Christ, your Redeemer, your Lord and your God. Behold, I came into the world not to call the righteous but sinners to repentance; the whole need no physician, but they that are sick; wherefore, **little children are**

whole, for they are not capable of committing sin; wherefore the curse of Adam is taken from them in me, that it hath no power over them; And their little children need no repentance, neither baptism (Moroni 8:8, 11).

This same Jesus said:

"Verily I say unto you, Except ye be converted, and become as little children, ye shall not enter into the kingdom of heaven. Whosoever therefore shall humble himself as this little child, the same is greatest in the kingdom of heaven. And whoso shall receive one such little child in my name receiveth me. But whoso shall offend one of these little ones which believe in me, it were better for him that a millstone were hanged about his neck, and that he were drowned in the depth of the sea (Matthew 18:3-6).

There are no scriptures that support the baptism of infants.

If you haven't discovered by now that some important teachings of Jesus Christ have been lost, changed or forgotten, then stay with me for "the rest of the story."

CHAPTER NINE

THE SIGNS OF THE TIMES BEFORE THE SECOND COMING OF CHRIST

*I*n the next chapter I will cover the most important events in this world since the birth and atonement of Jesus Christ, the Second Coming of Christ and the Millennium, when he will reign on this earth for one thousand years. Unfortunately, although these wonderful events will bring worldwide peace, they will be preceded by terrible calamities. I feel compelled to devote this chapter to "the signs" that Jesus gave which would precede his "Second Coming." I hope you will see the reason for understanding the reality of the warning Christ has given and will be prepared both physically and spiritually.

Here is what Jesus Christ taught about his Second Coming:

And as he sat upon the mount of Olives, the disciples came unto him privately, saying, **Tell us, when shall these things be? and what shall be the sign of thy coming, and of the end of the world?** And Jesus answered and said unto them, Take heed that no man deceive you. For many shall come in my name, saying, I am Christ; and shall deceive many. **And ye shall hear of wars and rumors of wars: see that ye be not troubled: for all these things must come to pass, but the end is not yet. For nation shall rise against nation, and kingdom against kingdom: and there shall be famines, and pestilences, and earthquakes, in divers places.** All these are beginning of sorrows (Matthew 24:3-8).

And because iniquity shall abound, the love of many shall wax cold. **But he that shall endure unto the end, the same shall be saved. And this gospel of the kingdom shall be preached in all the world for a witness unto all nations; and then shall the end come** (Matthew 24:12-14).

For then shall be great tribulation, such as was not since the beginning of the world to this time, no, nor ever shall be. And except those days should be shortened, there should no flesh be saved: but for the elect's sake those days shall be shortened (Matthew 24:21-22).

Immediately after the tribulation of those days shall the sun be darkened, and the moon shall not give her light, and the stars shall fall from heaven, and the powers of the heavens shall be shaken: **And then shall appear the sign of the Son of man in heaven: and then shall all the tribes of the earth mourn, and they shall see the Son of man coming in the clouds of heaven with power and great glory. And he shall send his angels with a great sound of a trumpet, and they shall gather together his elect from the four winds, from one end of heaven to the other** (Matthew 24:29-31).

I could have quoted all of Matthew twenty-four as well as Christ's parable of the ten virgins in Matthew twenty-five, because Christ was emphasizing the conditions that precede his second coming. He wants each of us and our families to be prepared and he gave us this warning: **"Watch therefore, for ye know neither the day nor the hour wherein the Son of man cometh"** (Matthew 25:13).

Does the fact that this prophecy of Christ's second coming is nearly 2,000 years old make it invalid or more difficult to believe? If you believe the prophecy, then you know he is still coming. We won't know the day or the hour, but we know the signs he gave of his coming: **"Wars and rumors of wars, nation shall rise against nation, famines and pestilences, and earthquakes in divers places, iniquity (wickedness) shall abound, the love of many shall wax cold."** You will note I have taken the liberty to summarize and emphasize those things for which I am going to give you current examples in this chapter. It is my intent to shock you into the reality of these signs and motivate you to make changes while you can still do so.

Some of these signs have been ongoing for 2,000 years. Are they more prevalent today than in the past? Is there any end to these calamities? Is there any human solution for them? We live in a wicked world that is out of control. You cannot listen to a newscast or read a newspaper today without being alarmed at the chaos and tragedy that fills the whole earth. When I started this chapter I found the following reports in our local newspaper, The Seattle Times. (Note the evidence of **"iniquity shall abound"** and **"the love of many shall wax cold."**)

Mexico City: "Fifty bodies found in Mexico, likely victims of rival cartel." More than 50,000 people have been killed in Mexico since President Felipe Calderon launched a military-led assault on powerful drug cartels in December 2005. (The most deadly violence in Mexico since the revolution–100 years ago).

Moscow: "Foes of Russian church say it's sold its soul to Putin." Many say Putin, who returned to the presidency last week, has used the church as a potent tool in his command structure, allowing it to amass vast riches in return for unquestioning support of his policies and spiritual blessing for his leadership. Under the atheist Soviet regime the church suffered persecutions with tens of thousands of its faithful purged, jailed or executed. The 1991 fall of communism opened the way for a renaissance that many celebrated as bringing Russia back to its spiritual roots. The church's leader, Patriarch Kirill, met with Putin and praised his two presidential terms as "God's miracle." In the Soviet era, Orthodox leaders infamously declared their loyalty to the atheist regime to allow the church to keep operating– and were enlisted as KGB agents. "We knew back in the 1990's that 90 percent of church leaders had been KGB agents," said Lev Ponomaryov, head of the respected For Human Rights group. The church claims 100 million Russians in its flock–more than three-quarters of the nation's population–though polls suggest that less than 5% of them are devout church goers."

United States: "Heads start to roll over JP Morgan's $2B (billion) debacle." The CEO, Jamie Dimon, said, "We made a terrible, egregious mistake and there's almost no excuse for it." He then added that the bank was "sloppy" and "stupid." He was referring to the surprise trading losses at the nation's largest and most respected bank. Another newspaper article said: **"Bad bet a**

reminder of 2008 meltdown." "The bad trades that caused JPMorgan's loss recalled the type of complex, highly speculative strategies that helped to nearly crater the global banking industry in 2008–before American taxpayers stepped in with a bailout."

United States: "America's export economy: arming and fattening the world." With the economy still struggling and the debates over how to fix the problem more intense– President Obama said, "I want us to sell stuff." The Washington Post reported: "The Obama administration is crafting a proposal that would make it easier to export firearms and other weapons." America has become the true "Lord of War" as the arms dealer motto goes. We are the leading arms supplier to the developing world and we are responsible for the majority of all weapons sales across the globe. Yes, we are so committed to selling the instruments of death to the rest of the planet that military industries have almost tripled their share of the U. S. economy in just a decade." ("In 2010 it was reported that the U.S. was selling $60 billion of weapons to Saudi Arabia. That's how Iran became a military power. We did the same to Afghan militants (later became Taliban). We repeatedly provide weapons to repressive regimes.")

That is what was reported in one day in our daily newspaper, and from these reports it is apparent that "iniquity shall abound." And I never included the "wars and rumors of wars." Imagine how disturbing and depressing the news would be if there was a daily report of deaths and the cost of the many wars and conflicts all over the world, as well as "the rumors of wars." And then we have "Natural Disasters," but are they "natural?" A columnist recently said how humbling Mother Nature was," but is it Mother Nature or the God of this universe? Are we humbled or just troubled and confused?

For many years I have been collecting articles about "The Signs of the Times," which are included in Matthew chapter 24. I would encourage you to do the same. As I list the present "great tribulations," I hope you will be alarmed and compelled to believe in the words of Christ. It is time to prepare and protect your family before things get worse.

MY LIST OF "THE SIGNS OF THE TIMES" (See details in Appendix 1)

"Wars and rumors of wars" and worldwide terrorism: Iraq, Afghanistan, Syria, Libya, Egypt, Israel, Palestine, Iran, Yemen, Pakistan, Somalia, (African nations), North Korea, United States (September 11, 2001 terrorist attack)

"Famines, pestilences, and earthquakes in diverse places" also tornadoes, tsunamis, floods, droughts, fires. "The world has entered a new era of catastrophes. Economic losses from hurricanes, earthquakes and resulting tsunamis, floods, wildfires and other natural disasters increased from $528 billion (1981-1990 to more than $1.2 trillion over the period 2001-2010. The worldwide economic cost of disasters in 2011 was the highest in history with a price tag of at least $380 billion. (The Washington Post, September 15, 2011).

Haiti had a 7.0 earthquake in 2010, Indonesia had an earthquake and tsunami in 2010, New Zealand had a 7.0 earthquake in 2011, and Japan had an 8.9 earthquake and tsunami in 2011. United States: Hurricane Katrina in 2005 was one of the worst in the history of the U. S. Super storm Sandy… Tornados in 2011 – 241 tornadoes in three days in 14 states. Droughts in 32 states in 2012.

"Iniquity shall abound" – The recession in the United States which began in 2008 is the worst since the great depression and the cause was greed and corruption. $720 billion in write-downs and losses by financial institutions. $30.1 trillion in market valuation wiped out.

Before giving you the next quote about the Financial Crisis in the United States, I am going to introduce you to the author, Henry K. (Bud) Hebeler. I met Bud Hebeler in 1977. He was seriously investigating The Church of Jesus Christ of Latter-day Saints. He had three degrees from M. I. T. and was the president of Boeing Engineering Co. and was being prepared to be the next President of Boeing Aerospace Co. I was asked to meet with him and I taught him everything you will find in this book. The challenging thing about teaching engineers is to teach them intellectually first and then let it filter down to their heart. Bud was not only a great administrator, he was a great student. He had a desire to know the truth and the integrity to do what was necessary to obtain it. He read, he prayed and he applied what he learned and when he knew it was true he was baptized and was ready to serve.

When Bud retired from Boeing he became interested in retirement planning. "Leaving Boeing, he embarked on a campaign to educate America about retirement planning. Mr. Hebeler is the developer of analyzenow.com, widely regarded as one of the best Web sites about retirement finances. His Web site gets several thousand hits each day." (The Wall Street Journal, March 31, 2007) He considers this his mission, answering emails from users of the site, and works at it six days a week.

Here is what Bud Hebeler has to say about the financial crisis in America:

> In the last ten years, the national debt has been growing exponentially so that it now totals over $16 trillion and is well on the way to exceed $20 trillion in the next four years.

> To illustrate the magnitude of this staggering obligation, Bud in an earlier paper had divided the national debt by 80 million taxpayers. Today that would be $200,000 per taxpayer! At an assumed interest rate of 4% the annual interest would be $8,000, without any payment on the principal! (For four years in a row the budget wasn't balanced... talk about the huge increases...)

> Bud went on to say:

> We are very close to the point reached in Greece where their government defaulted on its debt and paid only 40 cents on the dollar for their bonds. Greek public unions are refusing to work at the reduced wages necessary to reduce their deficit. Their youth are rioting because so many can't find work.

> To balance our own budget so that the deficits would be zero, we would have to completely stop funding all of our government including the military and Congress if we did not make very large cuts in entitlements such as Social Security, Medicare and government pensions or increase income taxes by 50%. Even then, our elderly population is outstripping the working people so that even more radical changes would have to be made in future years. The same is true if we have to raise interest rates because the

interest on our national debt is so large. Note that Obama is planning on only reducing the deficit over the next decade (not in the first 2 years as he naively promised in the previous election.) In the meantime, our debt will continue to build to about $20 trillion in the next four years. How will they pay the extra interest on the extra debt? (Henry K. (Bud) Hebeler, November 2012).

The United States isn't the only country in the world that is in financial trouble. "The 2009-2012 European recession is part of the 2008-2012 global recession, which began in the United States. The crisis spread to Europe rapidly and affected much of the region with several countries already in recession as of February 2009, and most others suffering marked economic setbacks" (Wikipedia).

Now that is a summary of "The Signs of the Times." I questioned making the list so long, but why should I shorten it? I want every reader to know how serious conditions are so they can't ignore or dismiss them. This is the time we live in. These are the days that Christ and the prophets have warned us about. Do you think Christ would shorten the list or add to it? For those who believe me, perhaps this chapter will help you reach out and bring others to Christ and his gospel where they will find peace. These are the times that try men's souls. God knows us well. We are His children. I hope you will help your family and your neighbors find Him and the peace that comes through His Son.

Can things get any worse? If you believe what Christ and the prophets taught, and are aware of what is going on in the world, the answer is yes. So I ask you now, what are you going to do about it? You can't stop the wars. You can't stop the earthquakes, the hurricanes, the floods, the droughts, etc. You can't stop the crime, the dishonesty, the greed, the corruption. So what can you do? You can prepare your family and your neighbors for the effects of all of the above. If we can't believe because of "the word of God," (Matthew chapter 24) then the next best thing for us is to be compelled to believe because of the undeniable signs enumerated in this chapter.

Start now to prepare for every emergency that might befall your household. Learn to live within your means. Determine what your real needs are and distinguish them from your wants. Get out of debt and stay out of debt. (Only the government can temporarily get away with such insanity as spending more than they take in.) Start an aggressive and consistent savings program for the long run (college, pay off a mortgage, retirement) and for emergencies (loss of a job, sickness, accidents, disasters.) The millions who were without electricity and the thousands who were evacuated because of Hurricane Sandy know now how important it is to be prepared for mammoth disasters. Your emergency fund goal should be for six months income. Saving for retirement depends on your age and the retirement program of your employer. Your commitment depends upon your needs.

Pay your tithing. Remember the promise in Malachi 3:7-12. Most tithe payers say you don't pay tithing with dollars, but with faith. Remember everything belongs to the Lord and you can't take any of it with you. Perhaps you should consider your tithe as "fire insurance" before the Second Coming. Store a three month supply of food, water, and other basic needs. (If you need help devising a plan to do this, then contact a member of The Church of Jesus Christ of Latter-day Saints. They have had this counsel for years.) Remember this admonition from the Lord: "I, the Lord, am bound when ye do what I say; but when ye do not what I say, ye have no promise" (Doctrine and Covenants 82:10).

Do not despair. Christ promised: **"Peace, I leave with you, my peace I give unto you: not as the world giveth, give I unto you. Let not your heart be troubled, neither let it be afraid"** (John 14:27).

You will not find the peace you are looking for without turning to Christ. Ignoring what is going on around us will not make it go away and does not help us, our families or our nation. Adversity can cause us to "give in and give up" or it can cause us to turn to God for answers. This is counsel worth remembering: "They were slow to hearken unto the voice of the Lord their God; therefore, the Lord their God is slow to hearken unto their prayers, to answer them in the day of their trouble. In the day of their peace (when everything was going well) they esteem lightly my counsel; but, in the day of their trouble, (the whole world is now in trouble) of necessity they feel after me" (Doctrine and Covenants 101:7-8).

Remember again the scripture in the 24th chapter of Matthew:

Immediately after the tribulation of those days shall the sun be darkened, and the moon shall not give her light, and the stars shall fall from heaven, and the powers of the heavens shall be shaken: **And then shall appear the sign of the Son of man in**

heaven: and then shall all the tribes of the earth mourn, and they shall see the Son of man coming in the clouds of heaven with power and great glory. And he shall send his angels with a great sound of a trumpet, and they shall gather together his elect from the four winds, from one end of heaven to the other (Matthew 24:29-31).

If a modern prophet and apostle told you "These signs of the second coming are all around us and seem to be increasing in frequency and intensity," would you believe him? Would you tell your family and warn your neighbor? "While we are powerless to alter the fact of the Second Coming, and unable to know its exact time, we can accelerate our own preparation and try to influence the preparation of those around us."

CHAPTER TEN

THE SECOND COMING OF JESUS CHRIST AND THE MILLENNIUM

*T*he second coming of Jesus Christ has been prophesied of by prophets in the Old Testament and by Christ and his apostles in the New Testament. It is not an illusion or dream of fanatical Christians. As the apostles watched Jesus ascend into heaven after his earthly ministry, "two men stood by them in white apparel: Which also said, Ye men of Galilee, why stand ye gazing up into heaven? **this same Jesus, which is taken up from you into heaven, shall so come in like manner as ye have seen him go into heaven**" (Acts 1:9-11). The Apostles received a confirmation of what Christ had taught them about his second coming. On more than one occasion the Lord testified that he would come again. Jesus said to his apostles: "**For the Son of man shall come in the glory of his Father with his angels; and then he shall reward every man according to his works**" (Matthew 16:27). This is the Second Coming of Christ when he shall come in glory and power. The final signs of his coming will be seen all over the earth. This is what Christ taught his apostles:

…the sun shall be darkened, and the moon shall not give her light, and the stars shall fall from heaven, and the powers of the heavens shall be shaken: **And then shall appear the sign of the Son of man in heaven: and then shall the tribes of the earth mourn,** (it will be too late to change and prepare) **and they shall see the Son of man coming in the clouds of heaven with power and great glory** (Matthew 24:29-31).

The Apostle Paul wrote about Christ's second coming to the members of Christ's church in Thessalonica:

> But I would not have you to be ignorant, brethren, concerning them which are asleep, (dead) that ye sorrow not, even as others which have no hope. For **if we believe that Jesus died and rose again, even so them also which sleep in Jesus will God bring with him.** For this we say unto you by the word of the Lord, that we which are alive and remain unto the coming of the Lord shall not prevent them which are asleep (dead). **For the Lord himself shall descend from heaven** with a shout, with the voice of an archangel, and with the trump of God: **and the dead in Christ shall rise first**: (those righteous people in the Spirit World who believe in Christ and have been waiting for his Second Coming shall be resurrected). Then we which are alive and remain shall be caught up together with them in the clouds, to meet the Lord in the air: and so shall we ever be with the Lord. Wherefore comfort one another with these words (1 Thessalonians 4:13-18). Those words should be comforting to the righteous people on the earth.

Paul could have added what Christ said concerning the wicked people living on the earth when he returns:

> But of that day and hour knoweth no man, no, not the angels of heaven, but my Father only. But as the days of Noe (Noah) were, so shall also the coming of the Son of man be. For as in the days that were before the flood they were eating and drinking, marrying and giving in marriage, until the day that Noe entered into the ark, And knew not until the flood came, and took them all away; so shall also the coming of the Son of man be. **Then shall two be in the field; the one shall be taken, and the other left. Two women shall be grinding at the mill; the one shall be taken, and the other left.** Watch therefore: for ye know not what hour your Lord doth come. But know this, that if the good man of the house had known in what watch the thief would come, he would have watched, and would not have suffered his house to be broken up. **Therefore be ye also ready: for in such an hour as ye think not the Son of man cometh** (Matthew 24:36-44).

And how shall the wicked be "taken"?

> BEHOLD, I will send my messenger, and he shall prepare the way before me: and the Lord, whom ye seek, shall suddenly come to his temple, even the messenger of the covenant, whom ye delight in: behold, he shall come, saith the LORD of hosts. But who may abide the day of his coming? and who shall stand when he appeareth? for he is like a refiner's fire, and like fullers' soap: (Malachi 3:1-2).

> "FOR, behold, the day cometh, that shall burn as an oven; **and all the proud, yea, and all that do wickedly, shall be stubble: and the day that cometh shall burn them up, saith the LORD of hosts, that it shall leave them neither root nor branch"** (Malachi 4:1).

When Christ comes, the righteous dead, who are in the spirit world, will be resurrected and the righteous mortals will be caught up with Christ to avoid the destruction that shall fall on the wicked. This will be the beginning of the Millennium when Christ shall reign personally on this earth for one thousand years. I want to comment on which mortals will remain and be saved from destruction when Christ comes and the earth is cleansed. I believe they will be people of all faiths, Christians and non-Christians. They will be people who lived good lives, who are honest and just, and who have integrity and good values. These people will continue to live out their mortal lives on this earth after Christ comes again. Children will still be born during this thousand years and will be raised in righteousness. They will not die, but will be resurrected immediately when their mortal lives are over.

The gospel of Jesus Christ will be preached under the most ideal conditions, because "Satan is bound" and cannot influence these good people. The Church of Jesus Christ with the teachings of Christ will spread all over the earth and bless every nation. The "everlasting" covenant that God made with Abraham and his descendants will be literally fulfilled as "all nations are blessed with the Gospel of Jesus Christ." It will be just as the Apostle Paul taught: "For as many of you as have been baptized into Christ have put on Christ. There is neither Jew nor Greek (he could have said there is neither Israelite nor Gentile)...for ye are all one in Christ Jesus." They all become Christians. "And if ye be Christ's, then are ye Abraham's seed, and heirs according to the promise" (Galatians 3:27-29).

Everyone during the millennium will be invited to "Come unto Christ" and become a part of the Covenant people of God. No more wars, no more corruption, no more politics, no more poor, because the Kingdom of God will be the governing body on this earth for one thousand years and Jesus Christ will be the King. Now that is something to look forward to, if you can see beyond the hard times that precede it.

There is a further explanation of the events at the time of the Millennium in the 20th chapter of the last book in the Bible–The Revelation by John the Apostle. Here we learn more about the order of the resurrection. John declares that Satan will be bound for a thousand years and "...that he should deceive the nations no more, till the thousand years should be fulfilled: and after that he must be loosed a little season" (Revelation 20:3).

The righteous Christians who had died are resurrected "...and they lived and reigned with Christ a thousand years. But the rest of the dead lived not again until the thousand years were finished. This is the first resurrection" (Revelation 20:4-5). The righteous dead who believed in Jesus Christ will be the first to be resurrected. The wicked will not be resurrected during those thousand years.

"Blessed and holy is he that hath part in the first resurrection: on such the second death hath no power, but they shall be priests of God and of Christ, and shall reign with him a thousand years" (Revelation 20:6). The second death is being separated from God's presence forever.

"And when the thousand years are expired (at the end of the Millennium), Satan shall be loosed out of his prison, And shall go out to deceive the nations which are in the four corners of the earth, Gog and Magog, to gather them together to battle... and fire came down from God out of heaven, and devoured them" (Revelation 20:7-9).

"And I saw the dead, small and great, stand before God; and the books were opened: and another book was opened, which is the book of life: and **the dead were judged out of those things which were written in the books, according to their works.**

And the sea gave up the dead which were in it (those that died at sea); and death and hell delivered up the dead which were in them: (these are the wicked people who had to remain in the 'spirit world' for one thousand years before they could be resurrected) and they were judged every man according to their works" (Revelation 20:12-13). The 'spirit world' is referred to as hell because only the wicked are there during the millennium. They are the last to be resurrected.

"And death and hell were cast into the lake of fire. This is the second death" Revelation 20:14. These are the people who were deceived by Satan and his evil spirits and chose to follow them and they will have to live with them forever. The "lake of fire" is a symbolic expression, and only those who experience this judgment will actually know what it is like. It is no wonder more Christians believe in Heaven than Hell. Hell would be a terrible enough punishment if you had to live forever with Satan and his followers.

The Apostle John confirmed that all people would be resurrected including the wicked:

> Marvel not at this: for the hour is coming, in the which **all that are in the graves shall hear his voice, And shall come forth; they that have done good, unto the resurrection of life; and they that have done evil, unto the resurrection of damnation** (John 5:28-29).

In writing about the Second Coming of the Lord and the destruction of the wicked, I was reminded of the story about my sister-in-law, Donna. When she was a teenager, she was listening to the radio (that's how we got the latest news before television). A religious leader reported that the world would end on a certain day in the near future. This alarming announcement frightened her and caused her to question what she had done with her life up to that point. She didn't belong to a church and didn't attend one, she was just living without a purpose. The day of "the end of the world" and the second coming of the Lord came and went without any changes, much to her relief. However, she never forgot what bothered her the most about that day: "what had she done with her life?" She said it was the turning point for her. She visited churches with her friends, but she didn't find what she was looking for. She said they just didn't feel right.

Her older sister, Norma, (my wife) who was a member of The Church of Jesus Christ of Latter-day Saints, suggested she meet with missionaries from her church. She was a little hesitant at first, but she trusted this sister and agreed. She had stipulations about when they could meet and it turned out that Thursday was the only day and never on the weekends because that was when she did things with her friends.

About Wednesday she tried to get out of this meeting, but her sister explained that the missionaries had changed their schedules to accommodate her and so she reluctantly agreed. They addressed her questions about the Second Coming of Jesus Christ and showed her the scripture where no one knows when Christ will return except our Father in heaven. They taught her about the church that Christ established in the New Testament, they taught her about what happens when we die, they taught her about the Fall of Adam and the Atonement of Jesus Christ. Line upon line she absorbed what they were teaching her and as she read and prayed about it, she discovered for herself a feeling that she did not feel in other churches. She met with the missionaries weekly for several months before she was baptized. Even then she didn't feel like she knew enough to be baptized but was told that after baptism she would receive the gift of the Holy Ghost which would help her learn even more. She was baptized June 7, 1953 and has been a strong and active member of The Church of Jesus Christ of Latter-day Saints since then.

Each time I think of her story, I ask myself these question; what have I done with my life? Am I prepared to meet Jesus Christ? Will I be lifted up with the righteous at his coming or will I be one of the wicked that will be burned as stubble? Am I paying attention to the various signs of the times and using this time to prepare for this event?

Who am I? Why am I here? After death what?

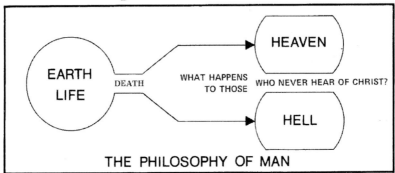

THE PHILOSOPHY OF MAN

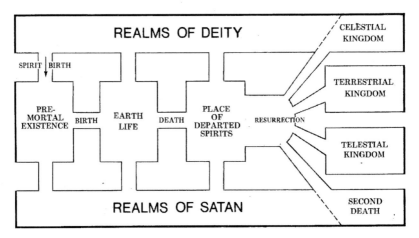

THE GOSPEL OF CHRIST ·· HIS PLAN OF SALVATION

1. WE ARE THE OFFSPRING OF GOD - Spirit Children of a Father in Heaven.
   Eccles. 12:7   Jer. 1:4-5   Heb. 12:9   Acts 17:28-29

2. WE CAME TO EARTH TO OBTAIN A MORTAL BODY AND PROVE OURSELVES. We left our Father's presence to learn to walk by Faith in God, our Father in Heaven, and in Christ our Saviour. We can know that Jesus is the Christ by the Holy Ghost and by living His Gospel we can return to the presence of Our Father in Heaven and have Eternal Life with our loved ones.
   Heb. 5:8-9   John 17:3   Heb. 11:1   John 14:26   John 15:26-27   Acts 2:37-39   Acts 8:12-20

3. AT DEATH THE SPIRIT LEAVES THE BODY AND ENTERS THE PLACE OF DEPARTED SPIRITS. Our Father in Heaven is just - The Gospel of Christ is taught to those who had no opportunity on the earth.
   Luke 23:42-43   John 20:17   Luke 24:36-39   I Peter 3:18-20   I Peter 4:6

4. RESURRECTION: THE SPIRIT IS REUNITED WITH THE BODY. This is the final judgment - Men are judged according to their works. Three Degrees of Glory. (Doc. & Cov. 76th Sec.)
   I Cor. 15:19-23   Matt. 27:52-53   John 5:28-29   Rev. 20:12-13   John 14:1-3   I Cor. 15:40-42

© 1978 Pugmire & Associates

CHAPTER ELEVEN

THE FINAL JUDGMENT AND THE THREE DEGREES OF GLORY

*T*his chapter will conclude The Plan of Salvation. God's plan for the salvation of His children is the gospel of Jesus Christ. We will discuss the "Final Judgment" and the "Three Degrees of Glory." I have included my own visual aid of this divine plan as a part of this chapter. As we review this wonderful plan, please keep in mind that no illustration will do justice to the real thing.

The top part of this visual aid illustrates what is being taught by most Christian churches today. Because it is not what was taught by Jesus Christ or his apostles, I have titled it **"The Philosophy of Man."** This philosophy has been taught by Christians for so many years that the tradition has sustained its validity. I do not understand how anyone could be comfortable with this interpretation of God's plan for saving his children. If at death there are only two places to go, Heaven or Hell, and if Heaven is reserved for only those who accept Jesus Christ as their Savior in this life, then Heavenly Father has pre-determined that many of his children will go to Hell because of where and when they were born. I am referring to all those who died without accepting Jesus Christ, many of whom never heard of him. The "philosophy of man" has no answer for how those who do not have an opportunity to accept Christ can be saved. I have been teaching these doctrines from the Bible for 60 years and from my experience most people want to believe what I have written in the earlier chapters of this book.

The second plan on the visual aid is titled "**The Gospel of Christ – His Plan of Salvation**" shows what we have discussed in previous chapters. Each part of the plan is summarized below.

Pre-Mortal Existence

We are all literal children of a Heavenly Father (God) and we lived with Him before we were appointed our time and place to come to this earth. We left the presence of God when we were sent to earth to get a mortal body and to prove ourselves worthy to return. Jesus Christ was fore-ordained to be our Savior and Redeemer.

Earth Life

During our earthly journey we temporarily forget about our Heavenly home. We are subject to the temptations of Satan and his evil spirits, who were cast out of Heaven for rebellion. We continue to have our agency–the right to choose good or evil. At some point we hear the gospel of Jesus Christ and learn what we must do to be saved. We learn we must have faith in Christ, repent of our sins, and be baptized and then we would receive the Gift of the Holy Ghost. These are the necessary steps to get back to the presence of God.

The Spirit World (The Place of Departed Spirits)

At death we will lose our mortal bodies and our spirits will pass into the Spirit World, where we will be greeted by loved ones in a joyful reunion. We will continue to live and teach the gospel of Jesus Christ to all, including those who had not heard it before. Jesus Christ went to the Spirit World after his death, to give all people an opportunity to hear his gospel before they are judged.

Resurrection

After three days in the Spirit World, Christ was resurrected. His spirit re-entered his body in the tomb, and he obtained a glorious immortal body which would never die again. He had overcome death and because of his infinite atonement, all of Adam's posterity will be resurrected. Some of the righteous were resurrected soon after Christ. "And the graves were opened; and many bodies of the saints which slept arose, And came out of the graves after his (Christ's) resurrection, and went into the holy city, and appeared unto many" (Matthew 27:52-53). Jesus Christ's resurrection was the beginning of the "resurrection of the just" or "the first resurrection."

Resurrection is the way **everyone** who has died will leave the Spirit World. The Apostle Paul taught:

> But now is Christ risen from the dead, and become the first fruits of them that slept. For since by man came death, by man came also the resurrection of the dead. For as in Adam all die, **even so in Christ shall all be made alive. But every man in his own order:** (note there is an order to the resurrection, everyone is not resurrected at the same time.) **Christ the firstfruits; afterward they that are Christ's at his coming** (1 Corinthians 15:20-23).

At the Second Coming of Christ all of the righteous who have died and are in the Spirit World will be resurrected. This is a continuation of the "resurrection of the just" or "the first resurrection."

This is also the beginning of **The Millennium**. "Then cometh the end, when he shall have delivered up the kingdom to God, even the Father; when he shall have put down all rule and all authority and power. For he must reign, till he hath put all enemies under his feet. The last enemy that shall be destroyed is death" (1 Corinthians 15:24-26).

The Millennium

When Jesus Christ returns he shall come in glory and power. The signs of his coming I discussed in the last chapter will have grown to such proportions that the whole world will be in turmoil.

The wicked shall be destroyed. Satan will be bound. Christ will reign personally on this earth with the righteous dead who are resurrected and the righteous mortals who will live out their lives in a world of peace. After one thousand years of peace and prosperity, Satan will be loosed for a season to deceive the nations before "fire came down from God out of heaven, and devoured them" Revelation 20:7-9).

The Final Judgment

> And I saw the dead, small and great, stand before God; and the books were opened: and another book was opened, which is the book of life: and the dead were judged out of those things which were written in the books, according to their works. And the sea gave up the dead which were in it; and death and hell delivered up the dead which were in them: (The wicked people who were left in the Spirit World for 1,000 years, then they were resurrected also) and they were judged every man according to their works" (Revelation 20:12-13).

Be not deceived, we shall be **judged according to our works,** but our good works will not save us if we don't have faith in Jesus Christ. The Apostle James warned us: "Faith without works is dead." He could have added: "Works without faith is dead." Remember these words of Jesus Christ:

> Not every one that saith unto me, Lord, Lord, shall enter into the kingdom of heaven; but he that doeth the will of my Father which is in heaven. Many will say to me in that day, Lord, Lord, have we not prophesied in thy name? and in thy name have cast out devils? **and in thy name done many wonderful works?** And then will I profess unto them, I never knew you: depart from me, ye that work iniquity (Matthew 7:21-23).

You will note I referred to this last section as "The Final Judgment." Actually "Judgment" and "Resurrection" are closely tied together. They happen at the same time. In the Final Judgment the wicked are resurrected and judged, this is "the resurrection of the unjust." They have no part in the "first resurrection" or the "resurrection of the just." "But the rest of the dead lived not again (were not to be resurrected) until the thousand years were finished" (Revelations 20:5).

Those who are just are resurrected after Christ's resurrection (Matthew 27:52-53), or at the time of Christ's second coming (Thessalonians 4:13-18) or during the Millennium.

The Three Degrees of Glory

Now I want to call your attention to the Apostle Paul's great explanation about different resurrected bodies.

I have already quoted from this letter of Paul to the saints (members of the church) at Corinth, where he was explaining the resurrection to them:

All flesh is not the same flesh: but there is one kind of flesh of men, another flesh of beasts, another of fishes, and another of birds. **There are also celestial bodies, and bodies terrestrial: but the glory of the celestial is one, and the glory of the terrestrial is another. There is one glory of the sun, and another glory of the moon, and another glory of the stars: for one star differeth from another star in glory. So also is the resurrection of the dead"** (1 Corinthians 15:39-42).

Paul compares the Celestial resurrected body to the sun which is the brightest. He likens the Terrestrial resurrected body to the moon, the next brightest. The third type of resurrected body is likened to the stars a lesser light in the sky. Paul is talking about three degrees of glory or three different types of immortal resurrected bodies. All of them are superior to our mortal bodies. Most people whom I have taught are quite comfortable with exchanging their concept of "Heaven or Hell" for "Three Degrees of Glory."

In another epistle to the Corinthian saints, the Apostle Paul spoke of being **"caught up to the third heaven"** (2 Corinthians 12:2), which would imply there were degrees or levels in heaven.

Jesus Christ said: **"In my Father's house are many mansions: if it were not so, I would have told you. I go to prepare a place for you"** (John 14:2-3). Another translation might be "In my Father's kingdom are many kingdoms."

I am now going to give you my opinion about who will be in these different kingdoms. There aren't specific scriptures in the Bible that answer this question. If at our time of a "final judgment" there was only Heaven and Hell, how comforting would that doctrine be? Can you imagine discussing what the dividing line is between going to Heaven or Hell?

Who will inherit the Celestial Kingdom?

Those who are valiant in their testimony of Jesus Christ.

Those who understand the call "Come Follow Me."

Those who not only believe in Jesus Christ, but believe Jesus Christ.

Those who believe Jesus Christ when he said:

Whosoever therefore shall confess me before men, him will I confess also before my Father which is in heaven. ...He that loveth father or mother more than me is not worthy of me: and he that loveth son or daughter more than me is not worthy of me. He that taketh not his cross, and followeth after me, is not worthy of me (Matthew 10:32, 37-38).

Those who keep his commandments. Jesus said: "If ye love me, keep my commandments" (John 14:15).

Jesus said: "But seek ye first the kingdom of God, and his righteousness; and all these things shall be added unto you."

Perhaps the simplest explanation will be this humbling declaration of the Savior:

Except ye be converted, and become as little children, you shall not enter into the kingdom of heaven. Whosoever therefore shall humble himself as this little child, the same is greatest in the kingdom of heaven (Matthew 18:3-4).

I do not believe Celestial candidates have to be perfect, but I do believe they are keeping God's commandments and trying to be perfect.

Who will inherit the Terrestrial Kingdom or middle degree of glory? In my personal opinion it will include:

Those who are **not** valiant in their testimony of Jesus.

Those procrastinators who are going to wait and see.

Those who are "luke warm" and are not "hot or cold" (Revelation 3:15-16).

Those who think they can serve two masters (Matthew 6:24).

Those who seek first the "honors of men" instead of the "kingdom of God."

Those who do the "right things" for the "wrong reasons."

Those who live the "letter of the law," but not the "spirit of the law."

Those who are more guilty of "sins of omission" rather than "sins of commission" (e.g. Keeping the Sabbath Day Holy.)

Those who don't live their religion seven days a week.

Those who are complacent about their Christian life.

Those who are hypocrites, e.g. professing to believe in Christ, but not following Christ. The Savior condemned hypocrisy when he was on the earth, do you think it will be any different on Judgment day? This list is long because I believe these are the things all Christians need to be concerned about.

Who will inherit the Telestial Kingdom or lowest degree of glory?

Those who are wicked and have chosen to be wicked.

Those who break the commandments of God and are not repentant of their transgressions.

Who will be cast out with Satan and not inherit any kingdom of glory?

Those who deny and defy the truth of the gospel of Jesus Christ after they have a testimony from the Holy Ghost and know it is true.

Jesus said: Wherefore I say unto you, All manner of sin and blasphemy shall be forgiven unto men: but the blasphemy against the Holy Ghost shall not be forgiven unto men. And whosoever speaketh a word against the Son of man, it shall be forgiven him: but whosoever speaketh against the Holy Ghost, it shall not be forgiven him, neither in this world, neither in the world to come" (Matthew 12:31-32). Remember it is by the power of the Holy Ghost we can know the truth (John 14:26).

Some further thoughts about our Judgment. When we are resurrected we are not going to be a Celestial person unless we have become one through our personal efforts to change and by the grace provided by the atonement of Jesus Christ. Each of us is becoming what we want to be. In each stage of life we have been given agency and are free to choose to become what we want to be. The conditions of earth life, with a knowledge of good and evil, provide an environment to "prove ourselves" while out of the presence of God. When we are resurrected we will remember our Pre-mortal existence and our mortal experience. We will know our Heavenly Father has given each of us an opportunity to hear the gospel of Jesus Christ at some time of our life, that is why each of us at the Day of Judgment will have to acknowledge Jesus Christ as our Savior regardless of how we have chosen to live:

> For to this end Christ both died, and rose, and revived, that he might be Lord both of the dead and living. But why dost thou judge thy brother? Or why dost thou set at nought thy brother? **for we shall all stand before the judgment seat of Christ. For it is written, As I live, saith the Lord, every knee shall bow to me, and every tongue shall confess to God. So then every one of us shall give account of himself to God** (Romans 14:9-12).

I have been teaching the "Plan of Salvation" for almost 60 years. I want to relate one of my most unusual teaching experiences. This is the story of Bob and Joan, a young couple I met when I served my mission in Wilmington, Delaware. My missionary companion and I were knocking on doors in their neighborhood in 1953 looking for anyone who might be interested in hearing our gospel message. A young mother came to the door and she let us in, but not for her benefit. She had her own church and she was a Christian. She was more interested in having us talk to her husband, who had his own ideas about religion, but didn't belong to any church. She suggested we come back when he was home. We did and we were surprised to find her husband was confined to a wheel chair.

He had polio when he was fifteen years old. His wife said they were going to put him in an iron lung and the paralysis miraculously stopped. Bob held a full time job and drove a car. He was a tall good looking man and was about my age (25). We immediately became good friends and our visits were long and intense.

When we taught him the "Plan of Salvation" it was always a question as to who was the teacher. He had already "worked out most of the details." He would say: "Don't tell me, let me tell you what I think." After he contracted polio, he had a lot of time to think about life and what it was all about. We were surprised at how much he knew. He never found a church that taught what he believed.

Bob told us, because of our meetings, he was having feelings which he had not experienced since he was seventeen years old. He said, back then he had a spiritual experience with prayer which he never forgot. He said he was having the same experience again and he didn't want to lose it. (It was the influence of the Holy Ghost.) He wanted to know everything and he couldn't get it fast enough. Our concentrated visits usually lasted four hours. In our second meeting he asked us if we realized the effect our message had on his household. He said he had not felt for years the peace and calmness that he was now having. After six months of meetings Bob and Joan were baptized. In the beginning it was Bob's interest that started this spiritual journey, but there were some "bumps on the road" and it was the faith, tolerance, perseverance, and love of Joan that kept this family together and on the road to salvation. They have raised a wonderful family. There are now fifty six members of their family and most of them are active in The Church of Jesus Christ of Latter-day Saints.

Most Christians I have met with are not comfortable talking about "Hell" especially when it is described as a place of burning and eternal torment. Nor are they comfortable believing there are only two final destinations: Heaven with God and Christ or Hell with Satan and his evil spirits. By now you must realize that much of what Jesus and his apostles taught has been lost or changed. After you have read all of these first 10 chapters and prayed about them you will know whether they are true or not, because your Heavenly Father wants you to know the truth and by the power of the Holy Ghost you may "know the truth of all things." It is my testimony to you that the Plan of Salvation I have described is the true gospel of Jesus Christ.

I feel impressed to address my family as I conclude this chapter. Will you seriously examine your lives and consider what I said concerning those I think will inherit the Terrestrial Kingdom? If you don't keep God's commandments you won't receive His blessings in this life or the next. There are specific blessings attached to each of His commandments. If you "pick and choose" the commandments you want to obey, then you may receive the blessings in this life for those commandments, but to inherit the Celestial Kingdom you must learn to keep **all** of Heavenly Father's commandments. "And, if you keep my commandments and endure to the end you shall have eternal life, which gift is the greatest of all the gifts of God" (Doctrine and Covenants 14:7). **I believe "enduring to the end" means being valiant in living the gospel of Jesus Christ until the end of the journey–the Judgment Day. Do not let procrastination, complacency or mediocrity lead you off from the path to "eternal life" in the Celestial Kingdom.**

CHAPTER TWELVE

GOD'S COVENANT PEOPLE – THE HOUSE OF ISRAEL

I would like to share with each of you my personal experience with the contents of this chapter. At age 23, I was called to serve a two year mission for The Church of Jesus Christ of Latter-day Saints. I had been in the U.S. Navy for two years and I had just graduated from the University of Washington with a degree in Business Administration. The Korean War was on and the Government set a limit as to how many young men could be called on missions because of the draft. Therefore, members who were not subject to the draft were being called to serve. Since I already had completed my U.S. military service, I accepted a missionary call to serve the Lord for two years.

I sold my Hillman Minx automobile to help pay for my mission to the Eastern States of the United States. (The mission included New York, Pennsylvania, New Jersey, Delaware, and Maryland.) My background in religion was pretty limited and my attendance in church had been sporadic during my college years. I attended Sunday School when I was growing up and knew some "Bible Stories." I had not memorized any scriptures and had some apprehension about sharing the gospel of Jesus Christ. However, I had acquired some social skills while attending the University of Washington and I was ready and willing to learn and to serve.

In those years of missionary service we received most of our training from missionary companions who had been on their mission for a while. (Missionaries always had a companion, they never worked alone.) Elder Robert Allen was my "senior companion" and he was an excellent missionary and trainer. In our first study class together he taught me the "House of Israel Story." I believe the lesson lasted 1½ hours and, for the first time in my life, I understood the "story of the Bible." He connected all of the Bible stories together into one single story and I got it! I will never forget that feeling.

I wondered why someone had not helped me see how this puzzle was put together before. I know some of you have had similar feelings. Reading the Bible can be like trying to put a jigsaw puzzle together when some of the pieces are missing or when the picture side is down and you only have the shapes to work with. I began to see clearly where all of these pieces fit together and I promised the Lord I would never pass up an opportunity to teach this "story of the Bible" to anyone who would listen. I believe I have been faithful to that promise and I never grow tired of teaching it. So now it is your turn, and I am thankful for this opportunity. I wish we could personally discuss this chapter. It will not be like the previous chapters where we talked about doctrine. There will be a lot of history, but that history will be important background for reading and understanding the Bible.

We are going to start in the Old Testament. Do not despair. I am going to give you an "overview" and most of what we need to know is in the book of Genesis. As you probably know, the book of Genesis was written by the prophet Moses. Moses lived about 1500 B.C. and he wrote about events that were 2500 years before his time, so you are not going to get all the information you would like. It is important at this point to define the role of a prophet. The prophet Amos in the Old Testament said: **"Surely the Lord God will do nothing, but he revealeth his secret unto his servants the prophets" (Amos 3:7).** Prophets are God's servants. When they speak as prophets, they speak for God. They reveal His will and His commandments. When these revelations from God are written down, they are called scripture. The "Story of the Bible," which includes "Bible stories," is recorded by prophets of God for all generations.

The first prophet on this earth was Adam. Adam walked and talked with God in the Garden of Eden. After he left the Garden of Eden, he still talked to God and was God's prophet for that period of time. After many years (generations) the posterity of Adam became very worldly and turned away from God and his prophets. The prophet Noah (2944 B.C.) preached for 120 years, but only his immediate family listened to him. The rest of Adam's posterity had "fallen away" from God, which is called an "apostasy." God caused it to rain and the flood washed them out of mortality. Of course you now know they didn't go to "Hell," they just entered the "Spirit World" together (1 Peter 3:18-20).

With Noah and his family (eight in total) we have a new "dispensation," meaning a new period of time when the word of God is dispensed or preached to his children by His prophets. The warning by the prophet Noah before the flood was an indication that God speaks to His servants the prophets for the good of the people who live at that time. However, it wasn't long before the posterity of Noah began to drift into apostasy and fall away from the counsel of prophets. They decided "to build a city and a tower, whose top may reach unto heaven." The LORD was unhappy with them and said:

> Go to, let us go down and there confound their language, that they may not understand one another's speech. **So the Lord scattered them abroad from thence upon the face of all the earth:** and they left off to build the city. Therefore is the name of it called Babel; because the Lord did there confound the language of all the earth: and **from thence did the Lord scatter them abroad upon the face of all the earth** (Genesis 11:4, 7-9).

Now I need to ask you an important question. Do you believe the Bible? If so, you now know that if God scattered these people **all over the earth**, then some of them came to the American continent. However, the history of those scattered to the American continent would not be found in the Bible, it would be a separate history.

Let us now return to the Bible history. The world was in need of another prophet and God prepared one. His name was Abram and later God changed his name to Abraham. I now want to give you a scripture, which may be the most significant in the Old Testament in understanding what and who the Bible is about from now on:

> Now the Lord had said unto Abram, Get thee out of thy country, and from thy kindred, and from thy father's house, unto a land that I will shew thee: And I will make of thee a great nation, and I will bless thee, and make thy name great; and thou shalt be a blessing: And I will bless them that bless thee, and

curse him that curseth thee: **and in thee shall all families of the earth be blessed** (Genesis 12:1-3).

God promised his prophet Abram and his posterity:

1. The land of Canaan (Israel today)

2. A large posterity (the House of Israel–God's covenant people)

3. **That through this large posterity God would bless all families of the earth.**

This covenant from God is what the rest of the Bible is about. With what would God bless all families of the earth? It is not spelled out in Genesis. Why is that missing? I want you to keep asking yourself that question as you continue to read. If I were speaking to you individually, I would ask you this question: "What is the greatest blessing God would want all of his children on the earth to have?" I have been asking that question for almost 60 years, here are the responses: "Salvation," "To believe in Jesus Christ," "To return to God," "To be saved," "To have Eternal Life." All of these answers are right. The Apostle Paul wrote to the members of the church at Galatia and said this about the gospel of Jesus Christ:

And the scripture, foreseeing that God would justify the heathen through faith, **preached before the gospel unto Abraham, saying, In thee shall all nations be blessed"** (Galatians 3:8).

The word gospel is a New Testament word, but it is being used here by Paul in an Old Testament setting. **The "blessing to all families of the earth" under God's covenant is the gospel of Jesus Christ,** which we covered in the first eleven chapters. The Apostle Paul wrote: **"For I am not ashamed of the gospel of Christ: for it is the power of God unto salvation to every one that believeth**; to the Jew first, and also to the Greek" (Romans 1:16). The gospel or the teachings of Jesus Christ are necessary for the salvation of all God's children no matter when or where they lived. You have to **have** the gospel of Jesus Christ before you can **share** it. The prophet Abraham and all other prophets had the gospel of Jesus Christ. They didn't just prophesy of Christ, they taught what he taught, because Jesus Christ is "the way, the truth, and the life: **no man cometh unto the Father, but by me**" (John 14:6). Was it harder to believe in Christ before he was born than to believe in him after his death? That's a good question, but there is no question that his atonement is available to everyone "**and in thy seed shall all the nations of the earth be blessed;**" no matter where or when they lived on the earth.

Do you know how long this covenant was to be in force? Forever!

> And when Abram was ninety years old and nine, the LORD appeared to Abram, and said unto him, I am the Almighty God; walk before me, and be thou perfect. And I will make my covenant between me and thee, and will multiply thee exceedingly. And Abram fell on his face: and God talked with him, saying, As for me, behold, my covenant is with thee, and thou shalt be a father of many nations. Neither shall thy name any more be called Abram, but thy name shall be Abraham; for a father of many nations have I made thee. And I will make thee exceeding fruitful, and I will make nations of thee, and kings shall come out of thee. And I will establish my covenant between me and thee and thy seed after thee in their generations, **for an everlasting covenant**, to be a God unto thee, and to thy seed after thee. And I will give unto thee, and to thy seed after thee, the land wherein thou art a stranger, **all the land of Canaan, for an everlasting possession**; and I will be their God" (Genesis 17:1-9).

God determines who will receive this great covenant. "And God said, Sarah thy wife shall bear thee a son indeed; **and thou shalt call his name Isaac: and I will establish my covenant with him for an everlasting covenant, and with his seed after him**" (Genesis 17:19). The covenant was be continued through Isaac:

> And the LORD appeared unto him, (Isaac) and said, Go not down into Egypt; dwell in the land which I shall tell thee of: Sojourn in this land, and I will be with thee, and will bless thee; for unto thee, and unto thy seed, I will give all these countries, and I will perform the oath which I sware unto Abraham thy father; And I will make

thy seed to multiply as the stars of heaven, and will give unto thy seed all these countries; and in thy seed shall all the nations of the earth be blessed;" (Genesis 26:2-4).

Isaac had twin sons, Esau and Jacob. Since Esau was the first-born, he was entitled to the birthright. However, he sold his birthright to his brother Jacob for a "mess of pottage." The birthright was the right or inheritance of the firstborn under the patriarchal order. This generally included a land inheritance as well as the authority to preside. This is not the only time the birthright will pass from the firstborn to another brother. There is a necessity to be brief in giving this history of Israel and I would encourage the reader to study the Book of Genesis for these "Bible Stories." Suffice it to say, the birthright or patriarchal right to preside now has passed to Jacob:

> And God appeared unto Jacob again, when he came out of Padanaram, and blessed him. And God said unto him, Thy name is Jacob: thy name shall not be called any more Jacob, but Israel shall be thy name: and he called his name Israel. And God said unto him, I am God Almighty: be fruitful and multiply; a nation and a company of nations shall be of thee, and kings shall come out of thy loins; And the land which I gave Abraham and Isaac, to thee I will give it, and to thy seed after thee will I give the land. And God went up from him in the place where he talked with him (Genesis 35:9-13).

The covenant was continued with Jacob. God called another prophet and surely the Lord will speak to his servants the prophets.

If Jacob's name had not been changed, his descendants could have been called "Jacobites." God changed his name to Israel, and therefore we call his descendants Israelites, which becomes the name of the covenant people of God who are direct descendants of Abraham, Isaac and Jacob. Those who are not of this line are called Gentiles, which is not a derogatory name, but just distinguishes those who are not Israelites.

The Prophet Jacob had four wives and from them came twelve sons. The twelve sons of Israel are literally the "house of Israel" (the family of Israel). These are the covenant people of God and they are the beginning (foundation) of the Twelve Tribes of Israel.

The favorite son of Jacob (Israel) was Joseph. "Now Israel loved Joseph more than all his children, because he was the son of his old age:

and he made him a coat of many colours. And when his brethren saw that their father loved him more than all his brethren, they hated him, and could not speak peaceably unto him" (Genesis 37:3-4).

His brothers were even more disturbed by Joseph's dreams. In them, he would rule over them and they would bow down to him. Their problem with Joseph was solved when they sold him to merchants, who in turn sold him in Egypt. This turned out to be the salvation of Jacob's household (the house of Israel) because Joseph became second in command in Egypt after he interpreted the Pharaoh's dreams when no one else could. God revealed to Joseph that there would be seven years of plenty followed by seven years of famine. Pharaoh believed Joseph and put him in charge of preparing for this terrible famine, which would cover Egypt and Canaan.

During the predicted famine the prophet Jacob sent his sons to Egypt to get grain. Lo and behold, Joseph's dreams of ruling over his brothers became a reality in Egypt. Joseph forgave his brothers and said:

And God sent me before you to preserve you a posterity in the earth, (the House of Israel) and to save your lives by a great deliverance. So now it was not you that sent me hither, but God: and he hath made me a father to Pharaoh, and lord of all his house, and a ruler throughout all the land of Egypt (Genesis 45:7-8).

"And Pharaoh said unto Joseph, …and take your father and your households, and come unto me: and I will give you the good of the land of Egypt" (Genesis 45:17-18). Jacob's family, the House of Israel, numbered seventy when they settled in Egypt.

Before the prophet Jacob died, he called his twelve sons together and said: "Gather yourselves together, that I may tell you that which shall befall you in the last days. Gather yourselves together, and hear, ye sons of Jacob; and harken unto Israel your father" (Genesis 49:1-2). He then gave each of them a blessing which pertained to their posterity, the twelve tribes of Israel. These blessings were prophecies of the future that were received through the Holy Ghost. Two of the most significant blessings were given to Judah and Joseph. Before reading their blessings I will quote from 1 Chronicles 5:2. This scripture shows why the blessings given to these two sons (tribes) were so important. **"For Judah prevailed above his brethren, and of him came the chief ruler; but the birthright was Joseph's."**

In the blessing given to Judah, Jacob said:

Judah, thou art he whom thy brethren shall praise: thy hand shall be in the neck of thine enemies; thy father's children shall bow down before thee. ...The scepter shall not depart from Judah, nor a lawgiver from between his feet, until Shiloh (Christ) come; and unto him (Jesus Christ) shall the gathering of the people be (Genesis 49:8, 10).

The prophet Jacob promised Judah that kings would come from the tribe of Judah to rule over all the twelve tribes. He also promised that Jesus Christ would be from the tribe of Judah. The Bible confirms this blessing given to Judah. The great kings David and Solomon who ruled over all twelve tribes (the Kingdom of Israel) were both from the tribe of Judah. Mary, the mother of Jesus Christ was from the tribe of Judah.

The prophet Jacob gave this blessing to his son Joseph:

Joseph is a fruitful bough, even a fruitful bough by a well; whose branches run over the wall; ...The blessings of thy father have prevailed above the blessings of my progenitors unto the utmost bound of the everlasting hills; they shall be on the head of Joseph, and on the crown of the head of him that was separate from his brethren (Genesis 49:22, 26).

The fulfillment of this blessing is not in the Bible, because most of the posterity of Joseph would be lost with the "ten lost tribes" in 721 B.C. and their history is not in the Bible after that date.

I would like to remind you that the purpose of the covenant people of God, the House of Israel, was to "bless all families of the earth" and this was an "everlasting covenant." The role of those with the "birthright" was to preside with the "patriarchal right to the priesthood of God." This was the blessing given to the tribe of Joseph wherever they might be. I will have more to say about this later.

After the death of the prophets Jacob and Joseph, the Israelites remained in Egypt "And the children of Israel were fruitful, and increased abundantly, and multiplied, and waxed exceeding mighty; and the land was filled with them. Now there arose up a new king in Egypt, which knew not Joseph. And he said unto his people, Behold the people of the children of Israel are more and mightier than we:" The Egyptians were afraid the Israelites would join with their enemies so they "set taskmasters over them: ...and they made their lives bitter with hard bondage" (Exodus 1:7-9, 11, 14).

The Israelites endured several hundred years of bondage "And God heard their groaning, and God remembered his covenant with Abraham, with Isaac, and with Jacob. And God looked upon the children of Israel, and God had respect unto them (Exodus 2:24-25). God then raised up a new prophet to liberate Israel from bondage. His name was Moses. If you have seen the movie, "The Ten Commandments," then you will understand how difficult it was to take the Israelites out of Egypt. The covenant people were in a fallen state and were given strict laws to live by–The Law of Moses. They were not ready to return to their promised land of Canaan so they spent forty years in the wilderness learning to rely upon the Lord before the prophet Joshua took them into Canaan.

The land of Canaan was divided among the 12 Tribes of Israel and you will probably find that map in your Bible. You will note Joseph doesn't have a land with his name, because his two sons, Ephraim and Manasseh each have a tribe and a land. The tribe of Levi does not have a land, because they were given the Aaronic Priesthood as a tribe and were spread out among the other tribes. "And verily they that are of the sons of Levi, who receive the office of the priesthood, have a commandment to take tithes of the people according to the law, that is, of their brethren, though they come out of the loins of Abraham" (Hebrews 7:5).

This lesser priesthood was then called the Levitical Priesthood, because the sons of Levi were given that responsibility. Perhaps this could be viewed as discrimination among the other Israelites who are all part of the covenant people of God, but of course it's God's Priesthood and He has every right to decide who should hold it.

The Israelites remain united under the rule of the judges and the great Kings of Israel: Saul, David and Solomon. Under King Solomon, Israel reached its greatest height as a nation. Israel was extended to the borders that the Lord had promised Abraham. "And God gave Solomon wisdom and understanding exceeding much, and largeness of heart,...And there came of all people to hear the wisdom of Solomon, from all kings of the earth, which had heard of his wisdom" (1 Kings 4:29, 34).

With this wisdom from God, King Solomon had peace and prosperity. He also built a magnificent temple. "And behold, I purpose to build an house unto the name of the LORD my God, as the LORD spake unto David my father, saying, Thy son, whom I will set upon thy throne in thy room, he shall build an house unto my name" (1 Kings 5:5).

After King Solomon's death, his son Rehoboam became King and, because he lacked the wisdom of his father and taxed the people too heavily, the northern tribes revolted and the Kingdom of Israel was divided in 975 B.C. Rehoboam was king over the southern kingdom, which primarily consisted of the tribe of Judah and part of the tribe of Benjamin and was called the Kingdom of Judah. The northern kingdom was called the Kingdom of Israel and was made up of the other ten tribes. Their king was Jeroboam who was from the tribe of Ephraim. This kingdom was also called Ephraim, because the tribe of Ephraim was the dominant power.

The House of Israel, God's covenant people, were turning away from God and not following God's prophets. They were "ripe for destruction" and another apostasy. The prophet Isaiah warned Israel that the Lord would use Assyria as "the rod of my anger" if they did not repent (Isaiah 10:5-6). In 721 B.C. the northern kingdom of Israel was taken captive by the Assyrians (2 Kings 17:1-6) ending the known history of the ten tribes of Israel in the north. Eventually, many of these captive Israelites escaped into the north countries and became known as the "lost ten tribes." These tribes of Israel have been lost for 2,700 years. They have been mixed with the Gentile nations in the north countries, which means there are many Israelites in those countries who have lost their identity and origin.

All that remained of the great Kingdom of Israel under David and Solomon was the Kingdom of Judah. This kingdom consisted primarily of the tribe of Judah and part of the tribe of Benjamin, but later many members of other tribes came to the southern kingdom and became a part of the nation of Judah. "For the Levites left their suburbs and their possession, and came to Judah and Jerusalem:" (2 Chronicles 11:14). "And he gathered all Judah and Benjamin, and the strangers with them out of Ephraim and Manasseh, and out of Simeon: for they fell to him out of Israel in abundance, when they saw that the Lord his God was with him" (2 Chronicles 15:9).

Twenty rulers reigned over the Kingdom of Judah after the death of Solomon until the fall of Jerusalem and captivity of Judah by the Babylonians in 587 B.C. Only four of these kings over Judah were good spiritual leaders. God called prophets to warn the people, but they persisted in idolatry and wickedness. "And the Lord said, I will remove Judah also out of my sight, as I have removed Israel, and will cast off this city Jerusalem which I have chosen, and the house of which I said, My name shall be there" (2 Kings 23:27).

The fall of Judah and their exile to Babylon brought an end to the Kingdom of Judah and to the known Israelite Nation. (The known history of the world does not have a complete account of all of the twelve tribes of Israel. For example: What happened to the ten lost tribes?)

In summarizing the history of the covenant people of God, the House of Israel, what have we learned? Through wickedness and idolatry they lost their land (Canaan), they lost their freedom, most of them lost their identity (except for the tribe of Judah, the Jews), they lost their kingdom, they lost their purpose (to bless all families of the earth with the gospel of Jesus Christ), and they were scattered all over the face of the earth. Another complete apostasy silenced their prophets. When Jesus Christ came and was born among them as was prophesied by their prophets, who accepted him? Unfortunately, most of the tribe of Judah (the Jews) did not. After revolting the Jews were scattered in A.D. 70 by the Romans, completing the scattering of the entire House of Israel, God's covenant people, among all nations.

At this point in history it would appear as if God has failed because his people, the House of Israel, failed. Or is there more to the story? If you think this is the end of the House of Israel and the covenant that God made with them, then you need to understand, you only know the beginning of their story. I want you to consider what God promised the Israelite people: His covenant with them was an **"everlasting covenant"** (Genesis 17:7). It is still in force and it will be fulfilled.

God revealed to his servants the prophets that the Israelites would be scattered among all people on the earth. "The Lord shall cause thee to be smitten before thine enemies: thou shalt go out one way against them, and flee seven ways before them: **and shalt be removed into all the kingdoms of the earth." "And the Lord shall scatter thee among all people, from the one end of the earth even unto the other"** (Deuteronomy 28:25, 64). **"...I will sift the house of Israel among all nations, like as corn is sifted in a sieve**, yet shall not the least grain fall upon the earth" (Amos 9:9). God knew His covenant people were going to be scattered and there was a purpose in this. You will know His purpose when you read the rest of the story.

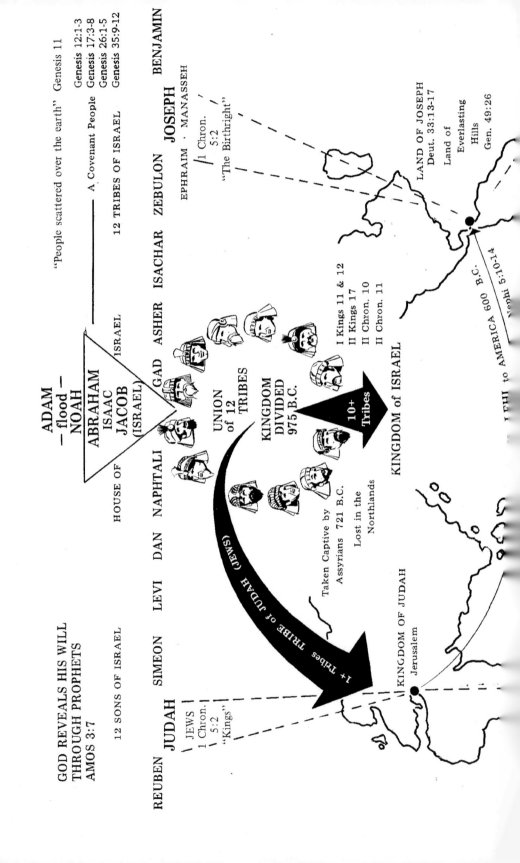

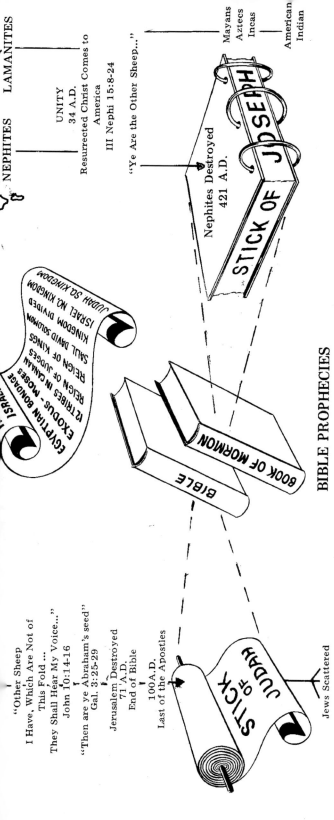

BIBLE PROPHECIES

EZEKIEL 37:15-21 The Stick of Judah (Bible) and The Stick of Joseph (Book of Mormon)

GENESIS 49 Israel (Jacob) blesses the 12 Tribes of Israel   GEN. 49:1,2   II Nephi 3:12   "That which shall befall you in the last days."

GEN. 49:8-12   Blessing of Judah (Jews) - fulfillment found in the Bible

GEN. 49:22-26   Blessing of Joseph (Descendants of Joseph) - fulfillment found in Book of Mormon

DEUTERONOMY 33:13-17   Moses blesses the 12 Tribes - Land of Joseph (America) described

ISAIAH 29   A voice from the dust...a marvelous work and a wonder to come from God...through an unlearned man...a sealed book...at a time when the world is in confusion and darkness...because of no prophets.

THE BIBLE AND THE BOOK OF MORMON

Pugmire/Christenson © 1987

NEPHITES & LAMANITES

UNITY
34 A.D.
Resurrected Christ Comes to America
III Nephi 15:8-24
"Ye Are the Other Sheep..."

Mayans
Aztecs
Incas

American Indian

Nephites Destroyed
421 A.D.

STICK OF JOSEPH

ISRAEL

EGYPTIAN BONDAGE
EXODUS - MOSES
12 TRIBES IN CANAAN
REIGN OF JUDGES
REIGN OF KINGS
SAUL DAVID SOLOMON
KINGDOM DIVIDED
ISRAEL NO. KINGDOM
JUDAH SO. KINGDOM

BOOK OF MORMON

BIBLE

STICK OF JUDAH

Jews Scattered

"Other Sheep I Have, Which Are Not of This Fold ... They Shall Hear My Voice..."
John 10:14-16

"Then are ye Abraham's seed"
Gal. 3:25-29

Jerusalem Destroyed
71 A.D.
End of Bible

100 A.D.
Last of the Apostles

CHAPTER THIRTEEN

OTHER ISRAELITES FROM THE TRIBE OF JOSEPH

$\mathcal{T}$he last chapter on the House of Israel was rather long, but I think **all of the information in that chapter is important in order to read and understand the** Bible. It may help when you review the House of Israel story to refer to the visual aid at the end of chapter 12. I created this teaching aid to help people understand the history of the House of Israel in the Bible and to introduce The Book of Mormon as a part of Bible history.

In 1965 I was asked by our bishop to visit a family who showed up at church one Sunday. JoAnn was a member of the church, but her husband, Ross, was not. Some years before, at the time they were married, Ross had promised JoAnn he would listen to our missionaries sometime. He was now going to fulfill that promise, but he had several conditions. When I found out what they were, I told him, "We may only have one visit, because if what I tell you today isn't important enough for you to invite me back then we may not meet again." I taught him what I have taught you in the previous chapter–the House of Israel story. He was so excited about what he learned that we met for six months. Later Ross said, "Kay agreed to teach me from the Bible and our discussion ensued. I was amazed! No one had ever shown me the truths Kay taught me about the House of Israel."

Ross was a "sponge" and soaked up every session. His enthusiasm was contagious and he shared what he was learning with anyone who would listen. He was impressed to find that the Book of Mormon was part of the House of Israel story. His life began to change when he discovered that he too could become a part of the covenant people of God. "For as many of you as have been baptized into Christ have put on Christ. And if ye be Christ's then are ye "Abraham's seed, and heirs according to the promise" (Galatians 3:27, 29). Nobody had ever told him that before.

Now we will examine that part of the House of Israel story which was written in America. We have learned that **"Surely the Lord GOD will do nothing, but he revealeth his secret unto his servants the prophets"** (Amos 3:7). One of those Old Testament prophets was Ezekiel, and here is what the Lord told him:

> **The word of the LORD came again unto me, saying, Moreover, thou son of man, take thee one stick, and write upon it, For Judah, and for the children of Israel his companions: then take another stick, and write upon it, For Joseph, the stick of Ephraim, and for all the house of Israel his companions: And join them one to another into one stick; and they shall become one in thine hand.**
>
> **And when the children of thy people shall speak unto thee, saying, Wilt thou not shew us what thou meanest by these? Say unto them, Thus saith the Lord GOD; Behold, I will take the stick of Joseph, which is in the hand of Ephraim, and the tribes of Israel his fellows, and will put them with him, even with the stick of Judah, and make them one stick, and they shall be one in mine hand. And the sticks whereon thou writest shall be in thine hand before their eyes** (Ezekiel 37:15-20).

The preceding scripture is hard to comprehend if we don't understand the "House of Israel story." Ezekiel is talking about one record for the tribe of Judah and another record for the tribe of Joseph. In the previous chapter we learned that the history of the Kingdom of Judah continued until 587 B.C. and the tribe of Judah (the Jews) continued until the coming of Christ. The Bible is a continuous history of Judah, or the "stick of Judah." Where then is the "stick of Joseph?" Where is the record of "Joseph in the hand of Ephraim?" (Ephraim was the son of Joseph) Because the tribe of Joseph was given the birthright, (1 Chronicles 5:2), their history would be as important as the "stick of Judah."

FAMILY CIRCUS / Bil Keane

5-22

"Besides the Bible, did God write any other books?"

READ EZEKIEL 37. 15-21
The "STICK OF JUDAH" is the BIBLE!
Would you like a copy of the "STICK OF JOSEPH"?

Perhaps you are wondering if this important prophecy regarding another Israelite record of scripture is still to be fulfilled sometime in the future. That question is answered as we continue to read the scripture in Ezekiel:

And say unto them, Thus saith the Lord GOD; Behold, I will take the children of Israel from among the heathen, whither they be gone, and will gather them on every side, and bring them into their own land: And I will make them one nation in the land upon the mountains of Israel; and one king shall be king to them all: and they shall be no more two nations, neither shall they be divided into two kingdoms any more at all:" (Ezekiel 37:21-22).

Do you understand that scripture? When was Israel divided into two kingdoms? In the previous chapter we learned that after the death of King Solomon, Israel was divided into two kingdoms in 975 B.C. After that division, the Lord told Ezekiel, that Israel would return to "their own land," the land of Israel, and they would no longer be divided. In 1948 that prophecy was fulfilled when, in one of the miracles of our time, the free state of Israel was created. Since that part of the prophecy has been fulfilled, the prophecy concerning the coming together of the two records of Judah and Joseph should also have been fulfilled—and it has been. God has, in these last days, brought together these two ancient records of scripture.

The "Stick of Joseph" or the record of Joseph contains a history of several migrations to the American continent. In 600 B.C. a prophet in Jerusalem prophesied that because of the wickedness of the Kingdom of Judah, it would be destroyed. (Jerusalem was destroyed in 587 B.C. by the Babylonians.) This prophet was an Israelite named Lehi. Under God's direction, he took his family and left Jerusalem, taking with them a record of their history, which contained part of what we today call the Old Testament.. In these records Lehi's family found they were of the tribe of Joseph; therefore their personal history would be a record of a remnant of the tribe of Joseph.

After they left Jerusalem, the Lord led Lehi's family to the American continent. Nephi, the son of Lehi, wrote: "Wherefore, he said it must needs be that we should be led with one accord into the land of promise, **unto the fulfilling of the word of the Lord, that**

we should be scattered upon all the face of the earth" (1 Nephi 10:13). Remember this scripture in the Bible? "And the Lord shall scatter thee among all people, from the one end of the earth even unto the other" ('Deuteronomy 28:64). Surely, "one end of the earth even unto the other" would include the American continent.

The prophet Lehi said concerning this land (America):

> ...we have obtained a land of promise, a land which is choice above all other lands; a land which the Lord God hath covenanted with me should be a land for the inheritance of my seed. Yea, the Lord hath covenanted this land unto me, and to my children forever, and also all those who should be led out of other countries by the hand of the Lord. ...Wherefore, this land is consecrated unto him whom he shall bring. And if it so be that they shall serve him according to the commandments which he hath given, it shall be a land of liberty unto them; wherefore, they shall never be brought down into captivity; if so, it shall be because of iniquity; for if iniquity shall abound cursed shall be the land for their sakes, but unto the righteous it shall be blessed forever" (2 Nephi 1:5, 7).

Lehi's family were Israelites who lived the Law of Moses and were taught by prophets about the coming of Jesus Christ. Nephi, quoting his father, the prophet Lehi, said concerning the Jews:

> ... after they should be destroyed, even that great city Jerusalem, and many be carried away captive into Babylon, according to the own due time of the Lord, they should return again, yea, even be brought back out of captivity; and after they should be brought back out of captivity they should possess again the land of their inheritance. Yea, even six hundred years from the time that my father left Jerusalem, a prophet would the Lord God raise up among the Jews–even a Messiah, or, in other words, a Savior of the world. And he also spake concerning the prophets, how great a number had testified of these things, concerning this Messiah, of whom he had spoken, or this Redeemer of the world. Wherefore, all mankind were in a lost and in a fallen state, and ever would be save they should rely on this Redeemer (1 Nephi 10:3-6).

The record kept by these Israelites would become a second witness for Jesus Christ, the Bible being the first witness. The Bible and the Book of Mormon fulfill the Lord's "law of witnesses:" "In the mouth of two witnesses shall every word be established" (2nd Corinthians 13:1). When finished, this record would cover one thousand years from 600 B.C. to A.D. 421 and include the record of an earlier migration of people from the Tower of Babel. (Remember this scripture: "Therefore is the name of it called Babel; because the LORD did there confound the language of all the earth: and from thence did the LORD scatter them abroad upon the face of all the earth" Genesis 11:9).

There is a significant scripture in the Book of Mormon, that I ask everyone to read because it shows God loves all of His children and speaks to them through prophets in all nations:

Know ye not that there are more nations than one? Know ye not that I, the Lord your God, have created all men, and that I remember those who are upon the isles of the sea; and that I rule in the heavens above and in the earth beneath; and I bring forth my word unto the children of men, yea, even upon all the nations of the earth?

Wherefore murmur ye, because that ye shall receive more of my word? Know ye not that the testimony of two nations is a witness unto you that I am God, that I remember one nation like unto another? Wherefore, I speak the same words unto one nation like unto another. And when the two nations shall run together the testimony of the two nations shall run together also.

And I do this that I may prove unto many that I am the same yesterday, today, and forever; and that I speak forth my words according to mine own pleasure. And because that I have spoken one word ye need not suppose that I cannot speak another; for my work is not yet finished; neither shall it be until the end of man, neither from that time henceforth and forever (2 Nephi 29:7-9).

Probably the most important event in this scriptural history is the visit to these Israelite people of Jesus Christ after his resurrection. First, a voice came from heaven that did pierce them to their very soul:

Behold my Beloved Son, in whom I am well pleased, in whom I have glorified my name—hear ye him.

And it came to pass, as they understood they cast their eyes up again towards heaven; and behold, they saw a Man descending out of heaven; and he was clothed in a white robe; and he came down and stood in the midst of them; and the eyes of the whole multitude were turned upon him, and they durst not open their mouths, even one to another, and wist not what it meant, for they thought it was an angel that had appeared unto them. And it came to pass that he stretched forth his hand and spake unto the people, saying:

Behold, I am Jesus Christ, whom the prophets testified shall come into the world. And behold, I am the light and the life of the world; and I have drunk out of that bitter cup which the Father hath given me, and have glorified the Father in taking upon me the sins of the world, in the which I have suffered the will of the Father in all things from the beginning.

And it came to pass that when Jesus had spoken these words the whole multitude fell to the earth; for they remembered that **it had been prophesied among them that Christ should show himself unto them after his ascension into heaven**.

And it came to pass that the Lord spake unto them saying: Arise and come forth unto me, that ye may thrust your hands into my side, and also that ye may feel the prints of the nails in my hands and in my feet, that ye may know that I am the God of Israel, and the God of the whole earth, and have been slain for the sins of the world (3 Nephi 11:7-14).

Now you know why we believe this sacred book is another witness of Jesus Christ. Christ came to the American continent and appeared to these Israelites because they were part of the covenant people of God. These are the words of Jesus Christ to his disciples on this continent: **"Ye are my disciples; and ye are a light unto**

this people, who are a remnant of the house of Joseph. And behold, this is the land of your inheritance; and the Father hath given it unto you" (3 Nephi 15:12-13).

He taught them his gospel so they too could do their part in blessing all families of the earth with the gospel of Jesus Christ. There was no contention in this land for 200 years after his visit. Then wickedness crept in and the people turned away from God. **Two hundred years later (A.D. 400) a great prophet named Mormon abridged the records of this people to preserve their history. His record is called The Book of Mormon and it was passed down to his son Moroni, who finished his father's record and buried it in the earth because of the wickedness and the destruction of his people.**

Moroni was the last prophet of these people. This is his testimony and promise to you when you read The Book of Mormon:

And I seal up these records, after I have spoken a few words by way of exhortation unto you. Behold, I would exhort you that when ye shall read these things, if it be wisdom in God that ye should read them, that ye would remember how merciful the Lord hath been unto the children of men, from the creation of Adam even down until the time that ye shall receive these things, and ponder it in your hearts.

And when ye shall receive these things, I would exhort you that ye would ask God, the Eternal Father, in the name of Christ, if these things are not true; and if ye shall ask with a sincere heart, with real intent, having faith in Christ, he will manifest the truth of it unto you, by the power of the Holy Ghost. And by the power of the Holy Ghost ye may know the truth of all things. (Moroni 10:2-5).

CHAPTER FOURTEEN

THIS IS THE CHURCH OF JESUS CHRIST

*T*he main message of the Bible is "For God so loved the world, that he gave his only begotten Son, that whosoever believeth in him should not perish, but have everlasting life" (John 3:16). This chapter describes how this message was to be given to the world. The covenant God made with Abraham, Isaac and Jacob and their descendants was to bless all nations of the earth with the gospel of Jesus Christ. This "everlasting covenant" was continued into the New Testament when Jesus Christ established his Church to carry his gospel to the world.

By the time of the birth of Jesus Christ, most of the people of the covenant, or the House of Israel, were lost. Ten of the tribes of Israel were taken captive in 721 B.C. and taken away into the north. Their history is lost to the world. Only the tribe of Judah (the Jews) and parts of other tribes remained in the Kingdom of Judah.

Among the Jews at the time of Christ were two influential groups: the Pharisees and the Sadducees. Neither of these two was accepted by Christ. The Pharisees were the "puritans" and more popular party and the Sadducees were an aristocratic minority. I hesitate to tell how to remember one of their major differences, but I can assure you that you will not forget it: the Pharisees believed in a literal resurrection, but the Sadducees did not and that was "sad you see."

Christ organized his own church among those Israelites who accepted him. The primary purpose for this church was to take his teachings, the gospel of Jesus Christ, to the whole world. The church was the means of fulfilling the covenant which God had made with

Israel. The Israelites would receive the gospel first, and then were to take it to the rest of the world (the Gentiles).

It is unfortunate that not all of the Jews were ready to accept Jesus Christ and his gospel, but those who did became the foundation of the Church of Jesus Christ. As we read about the organization of Christ's church in the New Testament, we need to ask ourselves if we really believe that Jesus Christ was perfect. As Christians, we believe that he atoned for everyone's sins and in order to do that he would have to be perfect, that is, without sin. Are we willing to extend that perfection to all of his works? When he organized his church for the purpose of teaching his gospel, was that organization perfect? I am not referring here to the people in the church, but to the specific positions or offices in the church which he organized. Could man do better than Jesus Christ in forming this important kingdom of God on earth?

This is the beginning of the organization of the Church of Jesus Christ:

> **And it came to pass in those days, that he (Jesus Christ) went out into a mountain to pray, and continued all night in prayer to God. And when it was day, he called unto him his disciples: and of them he chose twelve, whom also he named apostles;** (Luke 6:12-13).

Before calling his twelve apostles, Jesus prayed to his father for guidance. Therefore the apostles were "called of God" through Jesus Christ. He already had many followers (disciples), but these twelve apostles had a higher calling. They were special witnesses of Jesus Christ, and were the leaders of the Church of Jesus Christ on earth. **"Ye have not chosen me, but I have chosen you, and ordained you, that ye should go and bring forth fruit, and that your fruit should remain: that whatsoever ye shall ask of the Father in my name, he may give it you"** (John 15:16). These men did not choose to be apostles. They did not choose this important calling to serve. This was the Church of Jesus Christ and as the head of the church, Christ did the calling. In addition to calling the twelve apostles, he also ordained them, giving them the priesthood, or authority to act in the name of God. Those who accepted Christ and his authority would accept the apostles because Christ called them and ordained them.

These twelve apostles were common men with an uncommon calling. They had not been trained in the ministry, but they were called and trained by the Savior Jesus Christ. Jesus knew his time with them would be short so he told them God would send a messenger who would continue to teach them after he left.

"But the Comforter, which is the Holy Ghost, whom the Father will send in my name, he shall teach you all things, and bring all things to your remembrance, whatsoever I have said unto you" (John 14:26). This is how revelation is received from God. It comes from God through the Holy Ghost. **"But when the Comforter is come, whom I will send unto you from the Father, even the Spirit of truth, which proceedeth from the Father, he shall testify of me:** (That is how the apostles could know that Jesus Christ was the Son of God and the Savior of the world.) **And ye also shall bear witness, because ye have been with me from the beginning"** (John 15:26-27). The twelve apostles were special witnesses of Christ.

Jesus warned his apostles that they would be killed because of their calling in the Church of Jesus Christ. **"These things have I spoken unto you, that ye should not be offended. They shall put you out of the synagogues: yea, the time cometh, that whosoever killeth you will think that he doeth God service"** (John 16:1-2).

Then he comforted them with these words:

Nevertheless I tell you the truth; It is expedient for you that I go away: for if I go not away, the Comforter will not come unto you; but if I depart, I will send him unto you. ...I have yet many things to say unto you, but ye cannot bear them now. Howbeit when he, the Spirit of truth, is come, he will guide you into all truth: for he shall not speak of himself; but whatsoever he shall hear, that shall he speak: and he will shew you things to come. (That is prophecy.) **He shall glorify me: for he shall receive of mine, and shall shew it unto you. All things that the Father hath are mine: therefore said I, that he shall take of mine, and shall shew it unto you** (John 16:7, 12-15).

By revealing his will to the apostles through the Holy Ghost, Jesus Christ continued to be the head of his church after his death. In The

Acts of the Apostles we can observe the Church of Jesus Christ in action after the death of Christ. Luke, the author of this book, writes:

The former treatise (the Gospel of Luke) have I made, O Theophilus, of all that Jesus began both to do and teach, Until the day in which he was taken up, after that he (Christ) through the Holy Ghost had given commandments unto the apostles whom he had chosen (Acts 1:1-2).

After Christ ascended to heaven following his death and resurrection it was necessary for him to choose another apostle, to replace Judas Iscariot, who betrayed Christ and then went out and hung himself, leaving only eleven apostles in the Quorum of Twelve Apostles. The procedure for calling another apostle is found in the first chapter of The Acts of the Apostles:

And in those days Peter stood up in the midst of the disciples, and said, (the number of names together were about an hundred and twenty,) Men and brethren, this scripture must needs have been fulfilled, which the Holy Ghost by the mouth of David spake before concerning Judas, which was guide to them that took Jesus. For he was numbered with us, and had obtained part of this ministry (Acts 1:15-17).

Peter, the chief apostle, here tells the disciples that the betrayal of Christ by Judas Iscariot was prophesied of by King David in the book of Psalms. "Yea, mine own familiar friend, in whom I trusted, which did eat of my bread, hath lifted up his heel against me" (Psalms 41:9). King David knew this because the Holy Ghost revealed it to him. Peter continues:

Now this man purchased a field with the reward of iniquity; and falling headlong, he burst asunder in the midst, and all his bowels gushed out. And it was known unto all the dwellers at Jerusalem; insomuch as that field is called in their proper tongue, Aceldama, that is to say, The field of blood. For it is written in the book of Psalms, Let his habitation be desolate, and let no man dwell therein: and his bishoprick let another take (Acts 1:18-20). (Another Old Testament prophecy by the Holy Ghost was fulfilled.)

Then a new apostle is called in the Church of Jesus Christ:.

Wherefore of these men which have companied with us all the time that the Lord Jesus went in and out among us, Beginning from the baptism of John, unto that same day that he was taken up from us, **must one be ordained to be a witness with us of his resurrection.** And they appointed two, Joseph called Barsabas, who was surnamed Justus, and Matthias. **And they prayed, and said, Thou, Lord, which knowest the hearts of all men, shew whether of these two thou hast chosen, That he may take part of this ministry and apostleship,** from which Judas by transgression fell, that he might go to his own place. And they gave forth their lots; and the lot fell upon Matthias; and he was numbered with the eleven apostles (Acts 1:21-26).

The eleven apostles were promised they would receive revelations from God and Christ through the Holy Ghost. That is how a new apostle was chosen by Christ. Other apostles called later were Paul and Barnabas. (Acts 14:14)

Much of the New Testament consists of the letters of the Apostle Paul to different branches of the Church of Jesus Christ. The following quotes are from some of those letters where he emphasizes the importance of apostles and prophets in the Church of Jesus Christ.

I will quote from the epistle of Paul the Apostle to the Ephesians. Ephesians are people who lived in Ephesus, but note the way he addresses these who are members of the Church of Jesus Christ:

Paul, an apostle of Jesus Christ by the will of God, to the saints which are at Ephesus, and to the faithful in Christ Jesus:" (Ephesians 1:1). (Saints are members of the Church of Jesus Christ)

Now therefore ye are no more strangers and foreigners, but fellowcitizens with the saints, and of the household of God; **And are built upon the foundation of the apostles and prophets, Jesus Christ himself being the chief corner stone;** In whom all the building fitly framed together growth unto an holy temple in the Lord:" (Ephesians 2:19-21).

Paul likens the Church of Jesus Christ to a building. The foundation of a building supports and sustains it. The foundation of Christ's church consists of apostles and prophets.

The importance of those called to serve in the Church of Jesus Christ is emphasized in this scripture:

And he (Christ) gave some, apostles; and some, prophets; and some, evangelists; and some, pastors and teachers; For the perfecting of the saints (members), for the work of the ministry, for the edifying of the body of Christ: (the Church of Jesus Christ) Till we all come in the unity of the faith, and of the knowledge of the Son of God, unto a perfect man, unto the measure of the stature of the fullness of Christ:

That we henceforth be no more children, tossed to and fro, and carried about with every wind of doctrine, by the sleight of men, and cunning craftiness, whereby they lie in wait to deceive; But speaking the truth in love, may grow up into him in all things, which is the head, even Christ: (Ephesians 4:11-15).

The Apostle Paul here tells the saints that Christ has called apostles and prophets and others to teach them so they can be perfected in Christ. He also tells them Christ has called apostles and prophets and others for the work of the ministry in his church. If the members of the Church of Jesus Christ will accept these leaders and listen to them, they will have "a unity of the faith" and will not be "carried about with every wind of doctrine," which means they won't stray away from the gospel of Jesus Christ by following men's interpretations.

Now I am going to quote the Apostle Paul from his first letter to the members of the Church of Jesus Christ in Corinth. In chapter twelve Paul likens Christ's church to the body of a man. I would like to quote the whole chapter, but that is a little too much for this book. You may want to read this on your own.

"For as the body is one, and hath many members, and all the members of that one body, being many, are one body: so also is Christ. For by one Spirit are we all baptized into

one body, whether we be Jews or Gentiles, whether we be bond or free; and have been all made to drink into one Spirit" (1 Corinthians 12:12-13).

The body of Christ is the Church of Jesus Christ and after baptism the members are all Christians together.

"For the body is not one member, but many. If the foot shall say, Because I am not the hand, I am not of the body; is it therefore not of the body? And if the ear shall say, Because I am not the eye, I am not of the body; is it therefore not of the body? If the whole body were an eye, where were the hearing? If the whole were hearing, where were the smelling? But now hath God set the members every one of them in the body, as it hath pleased him" (1 Corinthians 12:14-18).

God has determined what parts of the body of man and the body of Christ (his church) are necessary. All parts of our human body have different functions and purposes and that is true of the different positions in the Church of Jesus Christ.

"And if they were all one member, where were the body?" (And if they were all apostles, where is the rest of the Church of Christ?) But now are they many members, yet but one body. And the eye cannot say unto the hand, I have no need of thee: nor again the head to the feet, I have no need of you" (1 Corinthians 12:19-21).

For example, the bishop can't say to the deacon, I have no need of thee. Why can't the bishop say he doesn't want deacons in the church? Because it isn't his church, it's the Church of Jesus Christ.

"Nay, much more those members of the body, which seem to be more feeble, are necessary: (it is not for men to say which positions in the Church of Jesus Christ are necessary) ...That there should be no schism in the body; but that the members should have the same care one for another." (There should be no division among the members in the Church of Jesus Christ.) (1 Corinthians 12:22, 25)

"Now ye are the body of Christ, and members in
particular. And God hath set some in the church, first
apostles, secondarily prophets, thirdly teachers, after that
miracles, then gifts of healings, helps, governments,
diversities of tongues" (1 Corinthians 12:27-28).

It seems to me if God has set apostles and prophets in the
Church of Jesus Christ, then both God and Christ believe they
are an essential part of his church. Actually, this next statement
by Paul is a summary of the whole twelfth chapter. In the first
twelve verses he is talks about gifts of the spirit, which are a
necessary part of the Church of Jesus Christ, and then Paul asks these
questions:

Are all apostles? are all prophets? are all teachers? are all
workers of miracles? Have all the gifts of healing? do all
speak with tongues? do all interpret? (1 Corinthians 12:29-30)

Paul doesn't answer these questions because they have already
been answered. Paul told us all of the callings or positions in the
church and all of the gifts of the spirit are necessary in the Church of
Jesus Christ. Here are other offices or positions that God has set in
the Church of Jesus Christ: Deacons (1 Timothy 3:7-13); Teachers
(Ephesians 4:11, 1 Corinthians 12:28); Elders (Acts 14:23, Titus 1:5,
James 5:14); High Priests (Hebrews 5:11); Bishops (Philippians 1:1, 1
Timothy 3:1-7).

It is unfortunate that the Bible does not give us the duties of all
of these positions in the Church of Jesus Christ. However it is very
clear that the most important calling in the church was that of
apostles and prophets. It is also very clear that all of these positions
must be "Called of God." A simple test is available to determine if
someone is "called of God." **And no man taketh this honour
unto himself, but he that is called of God, as was Aaron"**
(Hebrews 5:4).

Aaron was the brother of Moses, who was a prophet of God.
Therefore, this scripture could have been worded: No man taketh
this honour, but he that is called by a prophet of God. Therefore to
be "called of God" there must be a prophet of God called first.

What was the mission of the Church of Jesus Christ? It was the
same mission that was given to the Covenant people of God: "to

bless all families of the earth with the gospel of Jesus Christ." We find that emphasized by the Apostle Paul in his letters to the members of the Church of Jesus Christ in Galatia. He reminded them of that covenant when he said:

And the scripture, foreseeing that God would justify the heathen through faith, preached before the gospel unto Abraham, saying, In thee shall all nations be blessed (Galatians 3:8).

He also explained to them the purpose of the Law of Moses:

Wherefore the law was our schoolmaster to bring us unto Christ, that we might be justified by faith. But after that faith is come, we are no longer under a schoolmaster. For ye are all the children of God by faith in Christ Jesus. For as many of you as have been baptized into Christ have put on Christ. There is neither Jew nor Greek, (Israelite nor Gentile.) **there is neither bond nor free, there is neither male nor female: for ye are all one in Christ Jesus. And if ye be Christ's, then are ye Abraham's seed, and heirs according to the promise** (Galatians 3:24-29).

Baptism into the Church of Jesus Christ in the New Testament assured everyone they would be a part of the covenant people of God. They would become Abraham's seed and a part of the House of Israel. If they were Gentiles (i.e. not Israelites by birth) then they would be adopted.

The mission of the Church of Jesus Christ was to take the gospel of Christ to the whole world. Jesus ordained his apostles and said unto them:

All power is given unto me in heaven and in earth. Go ye therefore, and teach all nations, baptizing them in the name of the Father, and of the Son, and of the Holy Ghost: Teaching them to observe all things whatsoever I have commanded you: and, lo, I am with you alway, even unto the end of the world (Matthew 27:18-20).

However, Jesus' work on the earth was not yet finished. He said to the Jews:

I am the good shepherd, and know my sheep, and am known of mine. As the Father knoweth me, even so know I the Father: and I lay down my life for the sheep. And other sheep I have, which are not of this fold: them also I must bring, and they shall hear my voice; and there shall be one fold and one shepherd (John 10:14-16).

The Jews thought he was speaking of the Gentiles. However, Christ was sent to the Israelites, not to the Gentiles. On another occasion Christ said: **"I am not sent but unto the lost sheep of the house of Israel"** (Matthew 15:24).

What other Israelites were there? We have already discussed some: The ten lost tribes of Israel; a part of the tribe of Joseph who came to the American continent; and the Israelites who had died and gone to the "Spirit World." After his resurrection, Jesus Christ came to the American continent and visited the Israelites from the tribe of Joseph. He said to them:

Behold, the covenant which I have made with my people is not all fulfilled; but the law which was given unto Moses hath and end in me. Behold, I am the law, and the light. Look unto me, and endure to the end, and ye shall live; for unto him that endureth to the end will I give eternal life. Behold, I have given unto you the commandments; therefore keep my commandments, And this is the law and the prophets, for they truly testified of me.

And now it came to pass that when Jesus had spoken these words, he said unto those twelve whom he had chosen:

Ye are my disciples; and ye are a light unto this people, who are a remnant of the house of Joseph. And behold, this is the land of your inheritance; and the Father hath given it unto you. And not at any time hath the Father given me commandment that I should tell it unto your brethren at Jerusalem. Neither at any time hath the Father given me commandment that I should tell unto them concerning the other tribes of the house of Israel, whom the Father hath led away out of the land.

This much did the Father command me, that I should tell unto them (the Jews): **That other sheep I have which are not of this fold; them also I must bring, and they shall hear my voice; and there shall be one fold, and one shepherd. ...And they (the Jews) understood me not, for they supposed it had been the Gentiles; for they understood not that the Gentiles should be converted through their preaching** (Book of Mormon 3 Nephi 15:8-17, 22).

It was the responsibility of the Israelites to teach the Gentiles. They were to bless all families of the earth with the gospel of Jesus Christ. Christ established his church among the Israelites on the American continent. He then went to the ten lost tribes of Israel, but that visit was not recorded in The Book of Mormon or the Bible.

CHAPTER FIFTEEN

ANOTHER APOSTASY AND THE REFORMATION

Jesus Christ knew his apostles would be persecuted for preaching his gospel and building up his church. He forewarned them they would give their life for Christ and his church:

> **These things have I spoken unto you, that ye should not be offended. They shall put you out of the synagogues: yea, the time cometh, that whosoever killeth you will think that he doeth God service** (John 16:1-2).

His prophecy was literally fulfilled. With the death of the apostles, it was only a matter of time before there was a complete falling away (apostasy) of the Church of Jesus Christ.

The Apostle Paul testified of an apostasy:

> Now we beseech you, brethren, by the coming of our Lord Jesus Christ, and by our gathering together unto him, That ye be not soon shaken in mind, or be troubled, neither by spirit, nor by word, nor by letter as from us, as that the day of Christ (his second coming) is at hand. **Let no man deceive you by any means: for that day shall not come, except there come a falling away first, and that man of sin be revealed, the son of perdition;** (2 Thessalonians 2:1-3).

There were signs of this apostasy in the church while the apostles were alive. I quote from the Apostle Paul to the members of the church at Galatia:

I marvel that ye are so soon removed from him that called you into the grace of Christ unto another gospel: Which is not another; but there be some that trouble you, and would pervert the gospel of Christ.

But though we, or an angel from heaven, preach any other gospel unto you than that which we have preached unto you, let him be accursed. As we said before, so say I now again, If any man preach any other gospel unto you that that ye have received, let him be accursed.

For do I now persuade men, or God? or do I seek to please men? for if I yet please men, I should not be the servant of Christ. (I believe Paul is saying, if I preach what men want to hear, then I am not a servant of Christ.) But I certify you, brethren, that the gospel which was preached of me is not after man. For I neither received it of man, neither was I taught it, but by the revelation of Jesus Christ (Galatians 1:6-12).

The Apostle Paul also wrote the following to the members of Christ's church at Corinth:

For first of all, when ye come together in the church, I hear that there be divisions among you; and I partly believe it. For there must be also heresies among you, that they which are approved may be made manifest among you (1 Corinthians 11:18-19).

While there were apostles on the earth to put out the fires of dissension, the Church of Jesus Christ remained unified. With the death of the apostles, however, many of these new Christians began to "pervert the gospel of Jesus Christ." It was the beginning of what the Apostle Paul had warned:

For the time will come when they will not endure sound doctrine; but after their own lusts shall they heap to themselves teachers, having itching ears; And they shall turn away their ears from the truth, and shall be turned unto fables" (2 Timothy 4:3-4).

These new Christians were persecuted by the Jews and the Gentiles. They were oppressed by the Roman Empire from A.D. 64 (under Nero) until A.D. 313. Persecution was then replaced with acceptance when the Emperor Constantine declared Christianity to be the state religion in a political move designed to unify the Roman Empire. The apostles and revelation from God and Christ were replaced by Roman style Christianity dictated by Constantine, who was not even a Christian at the time. Constantine was the real head of this church. This new Christianity produced councils and creeds which changed both the organization and the doctrines of Christ's church.

The Emperor Constantine summoned a council of over 300 Bishops in the year A.D. 325 at Nicea. There, by vote (not by revelation), they attempted to resolve the conflict about the nature of God and Christ and their relationship. The result was the Nicene Creed. This was followed by the "Creed of Athanasius," which is a restatement of the Nicene Creed. I am going to quote a part of this creed (the full creed is in Appendix 2):

> We worship one God in Trinity, and Trinity in Unity, neither confounding the persons, nor dividing the substance. For there is one person of the Father, another of the Son, and another of the Holy Ghost. But the Godhead of the Father, Son, and Holy Ghost, is all one: the glory equal, the majesty co-eternal. The Father incomprehensible, The Son incomprehensible and the Holy Ghost incomprehensible. ...So the Father is God, the Son is God, and the Holy Ghost is God, and yet they are not three Gods but one God.

More councils and more creeds would follow: the Council of Constantinople in A.D. 38, the Council of Ephesus in A.D. 431, the Council at Chalcedon in A.D. 451. In all of these councils, men were still trying to define the nature of God and Christ. All of the creeds proceeding from these councils present God as incomprehensible and therefore unknowable, in spite of Christ's prayer to his Father, in which he said: **"And this is life eternal that they might know thee the only true God, and Jesus Christ, whom thou hast sent"** (John 17:3-5). This was an infamous period of creeds, confusion, and compromise.

Councils and creeds of men determined who God, Christ and the Holy Ghost were. Philosophical theologians debated the nature of God. They proposed and implemented their philosophical views of God and Christ and used their interpretations of scriptures to support those views. These creeds are confusing and self-contradictory, resulting in another mystery, which can't be explained.

Why should creeds which evolved 200 years after revelation from God had ceased become more important than the scriptures which Christians agree come from prophets of God. I have already given too much attention to Constantine, councils and creeds, but it is important to realize that a complete apostasy (falling away) occurred from the church which Jesus Christ established.

Following the Book of Revelation, which is the last book in the Bible are two important words: **The End**. Those two words are not part of Bible scripture, but they do imply far more than was intended. It is "the end" of apostles and prophets who presided over the Church of Jesus Christ as recorded in the Bible. It is "the end" to revelation from Jesus Christ and God to their church. It is "the end" of Bible scripture.

This was "the end" of light from above and the beginning of "the Dark Ages," also known as the "Middle Ages." During this period, which lasted for over 1000 years, civilization almost completely disappeared in much of western Europe.

After the apostles were gone, bishops and other officers were nominated by or served at the insistence of the existing authorities. The affairs of each church or branch were conducted and regulated by the local officers, so that a marked equality existed among the several churches, none exercising or claiming supremacy except as to the deference voluntarily paid to those churches that had been organized by the personal ministry of the apostles. Throughout the first and the greater part of the second century, "the Christian churches were independent of each other; nor were they joined together by association, confederacy, or other bonds but those of charity. Each Christian assembly was a little state, governed by its own laws, which were either enacted, or at least, approved by the society" (Mosheim, "Eccl. Hist.," Cent. II, Part II, Ch. 3:2).

"The rightful supremacy of the bishops of Rome, or Roman pontiffs as they came to be known, was early questioned; and when Constantine made Byzantium, or Constantinople, the capital of the empire, the bishop of Constantinople claimed equality. The dispute divided the Church, and for five hundred years the dissension increased, until in the ninth century (A.D. 855) it developed into a great disruption, in consequence of which the bishop of Constantinople, known distinctively as the patriarch, disavowed all further allegiance to the bishop of Rome, otherwise known as the Roman pontiff. This disruption is marked today by the distinction between 'Roman Catholics and Greek Catholics (James E. Talmage, "The Great Apostasy," p. 133).

In 1964 I went to a life insurance convention with Bill, a fellow insurance agent. He had been given a copy of The Book of Mormon and I told him I would like to talk to him about the relationship between the Bible and The Book of Mormon. This led to about six months of scripture study together. During this time another agent, who was Catholic, began to worry about Bill's spiritual welfare and arranged for him to meet with a Catholic priest at a local Catholic university. During the visit, Bill asked the priest about the infamous succession of popes during the Dark Ages. His response was: "That's our history." Bill already knew the history and was troubled by it. He wondered how any authority from God (the Priesthood) could have survived this history. Bill received a confirmation of what I had taught him about the great apostasy of the Church of Jesus Christ after the death of the apostles. An understanding of that apostasy was the preparation he needed for understanding the restoration to the earth of the priesthood and the Church of Jesus Christ.

I am now going to give you some of "that history." This will leave you with some doubts about whether Christianity during the "Dark Ages" was "Bible Christianity." For now, you may want to skim through it and be thankful for the Reformers who God prepared to change the corruption in the Church.

The Catholic Church believes their authority (priesthood) comes from the Apostle Peter and is continuous to the present Pope. I am going to quote from "The Intellectual Development of Europe" Vol. I, ch. XII by J. W. Draper:

> To some it might seem, considering the interests of religion alone, desirable to omit all biographical reference to the popes; but this cannot be done with justice to the subject. The essential principle of the papacy, the Roman pontiff is the vicar of Christ upon earth, necessarily obtrudes his personal relation upon us.

How shall we understand his faith unless we see it illustrated in his life? Indeed, the unhappy character of those relations was the inciting cause of the movements in Germany, France, and England, ending in the extinction of the papacy as an actual political power, movements to be understood only through a sufficient knowledge of the private lives and opinions of the popes. It is well, as far as possible, to abstain from burdening systems with the imperfections of individuals. In this case they are inseparably interwoven. The signal peculiarity of the papacy is that, though its history may be imposing, its biography is infamous. I shall, however, forbear to speak of it in this latter respect more than the occasion seems necessarily to require; shall pass in silence some of those cases which would profoundly shock my religious reader, and therefore restrict myself to the ages between the middle of the eighth and the middle of the eleventh centuries, excusing myself to the impartial critic by the apology that these were the ages with which I have been chiefly concerned in this chapter.

The author, J. W. Draper, then covers the history of Popes (the Papacy) from Pope Paul I in A.D. 757 to Gregory VI in A.D. 1045:

After such details it is almost needless to allude to the annals of succeeding popes: to relate that John XIII was strangled in prison; that Boniface VII imprisoned Benedict VII and killed him by starvation, that John XIV was secretly put to death in the dungeons of the Castle of St. Angelo; that the corpse of Boniface was dragged by the populace through the streets. The sentiment of reverence for the sovereign pontiff, nay, even of respect, had become extinct in Rome; throughout Europe the clergy were so shocked at the state of things, that, in their indignation, they began to look with approbation on the intention of the Emperor Otho to take from the Italians their privilege of appointing the successor of St. Peter, and confine it to his own family. But his kinsman, Gregory V. whom he placed on the pontifical throne, was very soon compelled by the Romans to fly; his excommunications and religious thunders were turned into derision by them; they were too well acquainted with the true nature of those terrors; they were living behind the scenes. A terrible punishment awaited the Anti-pope John XVI. Otho returned into Italy, seized him, put out his eyes, cut off his nose and tongue, and sent him through the streets mounted on an ass, with his face to the tail, and a wine-bladder on his head. It seemed impossible that things could become worse: yet Rome had still to see Benedict IX, A.D. 1033, a boy of less than twelve years, raised to the apostolic throne. Of this pontiff, one of his successors, Victor III, declared that his life was so shameful, so foul, so execrable, that he shuddered to describe it. He ruled like a captain of banditti rather than a prelate. The people at last, unable to bear his adulteries, homicides, and abominations any longer, rose against him. In despair of maintaining his position, he put up the papacy at auction. It was bought by a presbyter name John, who became Gregory VI A.D. 1045. (J. W. Draper, "Intellectual Development of Europe," Vol. I, ch. XII, pp. 378-381). (Also found in "The Great Apostasy," pp. 144-147) by James Talmage).

The thoroughly apostate and utterly corrupt condition of the Church of Rome as proclaimed by its history down to the end of the fifteenth century, was necessarily accompanied by absence of all spiritual sanctity and power whatever may have been the arrogant assumptions of the Church as to authority in spiritual affairs. Revolts against the Church, both as rebellion against her tyranny and in protest against her heresies, were not lacking. The most significant of these anti-church agitations arose in the connection with the awakening of intellectual activity which began in the latter part of the fourteenth century. The period from the tenth century onward to the time of the awakening has come to be known as the dark ages—characterized by stagnation in the progress of the useful arts and sciences as well as of fine arts and letters, and by a general condition of illiteracy and ignorance among the masses" (James E. Talmage,"The Great Apostasy" p.150).

Now you can understand why this period of time after the death of the apostles and the end of the Bible was so devastating to the church that Christ established. Christianity during the "Dark Ages" was not "Bible Christianity." We have to turn to secular history to understand how great this new apostasy (falling away) was:

By increasing changes and unauthorized alterations in organization and government, the earthly establishment known as "the Church," with popes, cardinals, abbots, friars, monks, exorcists, acolytes, etc., lost all semblance to the Church as established by Christ and maintained by His apostles" (James E. Talmage, "The Great Apostasy" p.141).

These changes were promoted and protected by the Catholic Church and lasted till the fifteenth century. Then some great men, who were inspired of God sought to reform the Church of Rome. This was the beginning of the Reformation, which was a revolution against the Catholic Church. The rebellion was almost simultaneous in England, Scandinavia, France, Switzerland, the Netherlands and Germany. These Reformers would become known as "Protestants," because of their protest against the Catholic Church. At first they wanted to correct the evils within the Church of Rome, like the selling of indulgences (paying for the forgiveness of sins in advance.) When their attempts to reform the Catholic church failed, they set up churches of their own (Protestant churches).

The fifteenth century ushered in the Renaissance or Revival of Learning. This revival was enhanced and fueled by the printing press. Johannes Gutenberg, a German printer, printed the first Bible in the 1450's. Almost 100 years before this, John Wycliffe, an English religious reformer, had begun a translation of the Bible into English. He believed the people needed to read the Bible to know what the source of their beliefs were. He was a "Bible Christian" and was persecuted for it. Wycliffe was known as "The Morning Star of the Reformation." He was openly critical of the Catholic Church and its teachings. His followers were called Lollards and, even though they were persecuted, they grew and helped spread the doctrines of the Reformation in the 1500's.

John Huss was a Bohemian religious reformer. He was ordained a Priest in 1401 and was an influential preacher. He read the writings of Wycliffe and translated them in Bohemia. In 1414 he was ordered to appear before the Council of Constance to answer charges of heresy. He was thrown in prison and condemned in a trial where he was not allowed to defend himself. He was burned at the stake in 1415.

Martin Luther led the Protestant Reformation in Germany. He also translated the Bible into German. In 1507 he was ordained a Priest in the Roman Catholic Church. In 1512 he received the degree of doctor of divinity and was appointed professor of theology at the University of Wittenberg. He gave lectures on the Bible and was a popular speaker. In 1517 he nailed a protest containing his Ninety-five Theses to the door of All Saints Church in Wittenberg. This protest was against teachings of the Catholic Church, primarily the sale of indulgences. The Pope granted letters of indulgences in return for money. (It was another way of taking care of your sins and avoiding repentance and confession.) In time the publication of Luther's Ninety-five Theses became a symbol of the Reformation, and the revolt against the Pope's authority quickly spread throughout Europe. By 1529 the reformers became known as Protestants, because of their protest against the despotism of the Catholic Church. Ironically, Luther became intolerant of any form of Protestantism other than his own.

It should be understood, Martin Luther had not intended to break away from the Catholic Church. He said:

I have sought nothing beyond reforming the church in conformity with the Holy Scriptures. The spiritual powers have been not only corrupted by sin, but absolutely destroyed; so that there is now nothing in them but a depraved reason and a will that is the enemy and opponent of God. I simply say that Christianity has ceased to exist among those who should have preserved it (In Galat. 1535 Weins IX P.I. 293, 24:27, p. 50, Luther and His Times, p. 509, Martin Luther, p. 188).

William Tyndale was one of England's leading Protestant reformers. He translated the New Testament from Greek to English. **He wanted to make the scriptures available to the common people and to expose the false doctrines and corruption of religious leaders.** He couldn't get the English translation published in England, so he visited Martin Luther in 1524 and was able to get it printed at Worms, Germany. He then had copies smuggled into England. He opposed King Henry VIII's divorce and was arrested. He was found guilty of heresy and was burned at the stake in 1536.

John Calvin was one of the foremost leaders of the Protestant Reformation in Europe in the 1500's. He was born in France and studied theology and law at several universities. He became dissatisfied with the Roman Catholic Church and took up the cause of the Reformation. He moved to Switzerland when his views concerning the Catholic Church were not popular in France. He corresponded with all of the great Protestant religious leaders of the time and was consulted on points of law and theology. He published many books which have influenced Protestant theology. He had a great influence on John Knox, who followed his teachings while carrying out the Scottish Protestant reformation. In 1561 the followers of Calvin separated from the Lutherans, the first great division in the Protestant Church.

John Wesley was a leader of the Evangelical Revival and the founder of the Methodist Church in Great Britain and America. His attempt to lead a Christian life through *method*, or discipline, was the heart of his spiritual growth. He preached in England, Ireland, and Scotland. He formed societies which eventually became the Methodist Church. He remained loyal to the Church of England, where he was an ordained minister, until the American Revolutionary War. He then recognized his differences with the Church of England and soon there was a separate Methodist Episcopal Church.

John Wesley understood the apostasy of Christ's church. He said:

> **It does not appear that these extraordinary gifts of the Holy Ghost were common in the Church for more than two or three centuries. We seldom hear of them after that fatal period when the emperor Constantine called himself a Christian. From this time they almost totally ceased....The Christians had no more of the Spirit of Christ than the other heathens... This was the real cause why the extraordinary gifts of the Holy Ghost were no longer to be found in the Christian Church; because the Christians were turned Heathen again, and had only a dead form left** (Wesley's Works, vol. 7, Sermon 89, pp. 26-27).

King Henry VIII in the early part of the Reformation declared his support for the pope and was rewarded by receiving the title "Defender of the Faith." Within a few years he was excommunicated from the Roman Catholic Church because of his desire to divorce Queen Catherine so he could marry one of her maids. In 1534 the British Parliament passed the Act of Supremacy, by which the nation was declared free from all allegiance to papal authority. By act of Parliament, the king was made the head of the church within his own dominions and thus began the Church of England.

The great Reformers were inspired of God. I believe they were foreordained from the Pre-Existence to reform Christianity. I believe if the world had been ready for apostles and prophets in the period of the Reformation, these great men might have been called by God to those positions. I believe these men are in the "spirit world" today and are unified in the Church of Jesus Christ. I believe they have resolved their differences because they have been embraced and taught by apostles and prophets who preceded them in death. I believe their calling in this life was to "reform" not to "restore."

If the reader will now look on the next page, a reprint from Life magazine, November 10, 1947, shows the results of the apostasy of the Church of Jesus Christ and the Reformation which brought about numerous Protestant churches. The initial opposition between the Protestant Reformers and the Catholic Church has extended to opposition among the various protestant Churches. Can all of these Christian churches be the Church of Jesus Christ? Who among them is a Bible Christian?

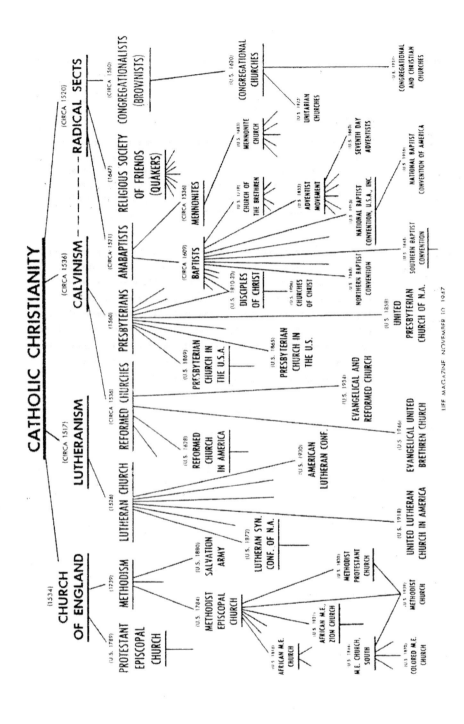

CATHOLIC CHRISTIANITY

CHURCH OF ENGLAND (1534)
LUTHERANISM (CIRCA 1517)
CALVINISM (CIRCA 1536)
RADICAL SECTS (CIRCA 1520)

LIFE MAGAZINE NOVEMBER 10, 1947

CHAPTER SIXTEEN

AMERICA - GOD'S CHOICE LAND

$\mathcal{T}$he Protestant Reformation was a confirmation of the Apostasy; it was the one thing that Protestants had in common. They believed the Catholic Church was not the Church of Jesus Christ, regardless of the Catholic claim of authority through their Popes.

Revelation from God through a prophet had been missing since the Bible came to an end about A.D. 100. The great reformers were inspired men of God, but they were not apostles or prophets. They never claimed to be. If they had, all of them would have been persecuted more than they were. They knew the church had departed from the teachings in the Bible, but couldn't agree among themselves as to the correct interpretation of those teachings and therefore we have this great division among Protestants.

This division among Protestants was the reason many people came to America. They wanted to escape religious persecution and they wanted more freedom. The Protestants got their name because of their protest against the Pope and Catholicism. Now, Protestants were protesting among themselves in this new land of liberty.

In 1948 I was stationed on the USS Philippine Sea at Providence, Rhode Island. I visited The First Baptist Church, which is the oldest Baptist Church in America. It was founded by Roger Williams, who was the minister in 1638. I was given a pamphlet entitled: "Historical Statement." I read with interest his banishment from one church in Salem, as Protestants protested against Protestants. He and others started another church. In the pamphlet was written:

They were devout Christians, but had broken away from the old ecclesiastical order, as many Christians in England were doing about that time, and here in the wilderness beyond hostile jurisdiction or fear of persecution, they established a new order which they had come to believe was in harmony with the teachings of the New Testament, viz., immersion on profession of personal faith in Christ.

I read with interest further:

In a few months Roger Williams withdrew from the Church, having been led to believe that owing to the corruption of Christendom, the rites of the Church had become invalid, And that there was no proper administrator and no proper church…"(Historical Statement by Rev. Henry M. King, D. D.)

Years later I found this actual quote by Roger Williams:

There is no regularly constituted church on earth, nor any person authorized to administer any church ordinance; nor can there be until new apostles are sent by the Great Head of the Church for whose coming I am seeking (Picturesque America, p. 502).

Roger Williams and the establishment of the colony in Providence, Rhode Island pointed out several concerns. No one had proper authority (the Priesthood), therefore these Christians turned to the Bible as their authority. This assumed authority was used to organize a church and to baptize new members. Churches did not accept each other's baptisms. Roger Williams recognized there was no authority to organize a church until God called new apostles.

In the early years of my business as a life insurance salesman, I met a young man who was in law school at the University of Washington. He was interested in talking about the Bible and it was the beginning of a great relationship. In his words, "You later became my trusted insurance agent and friend." We continued to meet periodically and I was surprised at what he remembered, because we could pick up where we left off six months before as if it were yesterday. He had a good mind and he was disciplined and a very dedicated Christian.

After he was married, my wife, Norma, and I met with he and his wife weekly for eight or nine months. We covered what is written in this book. When we were studying about the Church of Jesus Christ in the New Testament, he brought pamphlets from his church. He belonged to the Christian Church (Disciples of Christ). We were both surprised to learn his church believed there had been an apostasy from the church Christ established and there was a need for a restoration of the original church. Alexander Campbell, one of the founders of "The Disciples of Christ" said:

This movement has Protestant background and may be considered a movement within Protestantism...but they have gone beyond what most Protestants rely on. The Disciples seek to restore the church to its unity, purity, and vitality as revealed in the New Testament...with an insistence upon New Testament names, practices, ordinances and fellowship..." Thomas Campbell, son of Alexander, said: **"all divisions had been caused by departing from the simple teachings of the New Testament concerning the church and that the cure of all the evils of division would be found in a return to the teachings of the New Testament** (The Christian Life).

God's love and interest in His children did not stop when the Bible came to an end in A.D. 100. His prophet Abraham was given an "everlasting covenant" to bring the gospel of Jesus Christ to all nations of the earth. This covenant would be fulfilled in some future time. God and Christ were not dead. Although the church established by Jesus Christ was gone, apostles and prophets prophesied there would be a restoration. Here are the words of the Apostle Peter:

And he shall send Jesus Christ, which before was preached unto you: Whom the heaven must receive until the times of restitution of all things, which God hath spoken by the mouth of all his holy prophets since the world began (The Acts of the Apostles 3:20-21).

Christ will remain in heaven awaiting his second coming until the restitution of all things. The authority (the priesthood) will be restored, the Church of Jesus Christ as he organized it previously will be restored, and the gospel of Christ (the true gospel of Jesus Christ) will be restored. The Apostle Paul also taught of this restoration:

That in the dispensation of the fullness of times he might gather together in one all things in Christ, both which are in heaven, and which are on earth; even in him (Ephesians 1:10).

In the Old Testament the prophet Daniel, who interpreted King Nebuchadnezzar's dream, said:

And in the days of these kings shall the God of heaven set up a kingdom, which shall never be destroyed: and the kingdom shall not be left to other people, but it shall break in pieces and consume all these kingdoms, and it shall stand forever" (Daniel 2:44). **"...and filled the whole earth** (Daniel 2:35).

Christ established the kingdom of God, which was the Church of Jesus Christ, but that kingdom was destroyed and was given to another people. This is what Christ said to the Jews: "Therefore say I unto you, **The Kingdom of God shall be taken from you, and given to a nation bringing forth the fruits thereof"** (Matthew 21:43). Therefore the Kingdom of God that the prophet Daniel was talking about was to be at a different time, a later time than Christ's first coming.

This great event, the "restitution of all things" (restoration of all things) shall precede the Second Coming of Jesus Christ. It will be the preparation for his coming. God determines the "times before appointed and the bounds of their habitation" (Acts 17:26). He determines when Christ shall come back. He determines when his prophets shall be born and where they should be born. He determines when "all things shall be restored" and where they shall be restored. He determined when the Church of Jesus Christ would be restored and where it should be restored. He prepared a place where it would grow and "fill the whole earth" with the gospel of Jesus Christ. That place was America. God blessed the land of America.

The American prophet Lehi said:

…we have obtained a land of promise, a land which is choice above all other lands; a land which the Lord God hath covenanted with me should be a land for the inheritance of my seed. Yea, the Lord hath covenanted this land unto me, and to my children forever, and also all those who should be led out of other countries by the hand of the Lord. …Wherefore, this land is consecrated unto him whom he shall bring. And if it so be that they shall serve him according to the commandments which he hath given, it shall be a land of liberty unto them; wherefore, they shall never be brought down into captivity; if so, it shall be because of iniquity; for if iniquity shall abound cursed shall be the land for their sakes, but unto the righteous it shall be blessed forever (Book of Mormon 2 Nephi 1:5, 7).

When we examine the history of America, we see the hand of the Lord in the people who were brought here and what they accomplished. Columbus said, "The Lord was well disposed to my desire, and He bestowed upon me courage and understanding; knowledge of seafaring." Columbus acknowledged the hand of God in his life and in his preparation to sail around the world, which many called foolish. His answer was, **"But who can doubt but that the Holy Ghost inspired me?"** (Jacob Wassermann, *Columbus, Don Quixote of the Seas*, pp. 19-20).

Columbus discovered America had people living here, the American Indians, so he wasn't the first to discover this land. People had been here for many generations. Where is their history? Where did their ancestors come from? The Book of Mormon has some of their history.

The number of people who came to America to seek freedom of religion shows the importance and dedication of these people who had been persecuted because of their beliefs. America became a "melting pot" for many religious beliefs. Many came here because they wanted economic freedom or political freedom and a better life. They felt so strong about personal liberty that they were willing to fight for it and die for it. A famous statement by Patrick Henry, a statesman and a delegate to the First Continental Congress seems to epitomize the feelings of those settling in America. He said:

An appeal to arms and to the God of hosts is all that is left us! ...Sir, we are not weak if we make a proper use of those means which the God of nature hath placed in our power, ...**Besides, sir, we shall not fight our battles alone. There is a just God who presides over the destinies of nations and who will raise up friends to fight our battles for us. ...Is life so dear, or peace so sweet as to be purchased at the price of chains and slavery? Forbid it, Almighty God! I know not what course others may take; but as for me, give me liberty or give me death!** (*Life and Character of Patrick Henry by William Wirt 1816*).

The signers of the Declaration of Independence knew they were putting their lives in danger with the stroke of a pen. John Hancock warned his fellow delegates, "We must be unanimous; there must be no pulling different ways; we must all hang together." Benjamin Franklin replied, "Yes, we must indeed all hang together, or assuredly we shall all hang separately."

Who can doubt the hand of God during the Revolutionary War when George Washington led a rag tag army of sorts, which at its peak numbered 20,000 troops, against a well-disciplined English army of 50,000 men.

If we can believe that God has foreordained prophets for their roles in mortality, then it should not be difficult to believe that great leaders such as George Washington also were foreordained. His leadership, as a General in the American War of Independence and as the first President of the United States, was critical to this young nation. He was a man of God, who said: **"It is the duty of all nations to acknowledge the providence of Almighty God, to obey His will, to be grateful for His benefits, and humbly to implore His protection and favor"** (George Washington's 1789 Thanksgiving Proclamation).

The next miracle to occur after their independence was to unite thirteen colonies into a nation governed by a constitution. We, as Mormons, believe that God established the constitution through wise men who were raised up for that purpose. **"And for this purpose have I established the Constitution of this land, by the hands of wise men whom I raised up unto this very purpose, and redeemed the land by the shedding of blood"** (Doctrine and Covenants Section 101:80).

I am going to quote some of these "wise men" who God raised up to create the constitution and prepared America to fulfill its divine destiny:

Thomas Jefferson, who was the principal author of The Declaration of Independence and was the third President of the United States, said:

And can the liberties of a nation be thought secure when we have removed their only firm basis, a conviction in the minds of the people that these liberties are of the gift of God? That they are not to be violated but with His wrath? Indeed I tremble for my country when I reflect that God is just: that His justice cannot sleep forever; ... (Jefferson's 1785 *Notes on the State of Virginia*).

Benjamin Franklin, who signed the Declaration of Independence and the Constitution, said:

I've lived, sir, a long time, and the longer I live, the more convincing proofs I see of this truth: **That God governs in the affairs of men. If a sparrow cannot fall to the ground without His notice, is it probable that an empire can rise without His aid? We've been assured in the sacred writings that unless the Lord builds the house, they labor in vain who build it. I firmly believe this, and I also believe that without his concurring aid, we shall succeed in this political building no better than the builders of Babel** (Benjamin Franklin's request for prayers at the Constitutional Convention from the notes of James Madison).

These early American colonist leaders hoped for more help form God in their religious lives. They were aware of the many differences among the Christians who had settled in the thirteen colonies. The following quotes show a hope for a restoration of original Christianity.

Thomas Jefferson wrote this: Had the doctrines of Jesus been preached always as poor as they came from his lips, the whole civilized world would now have been Christian" ("In God We Trust" page 161 by Norman Cousins)

Thomas Jefferson had this opinion about Christianity during the 1700's:

> The religion builders have so distorted and deformed the doctrines of Jesus, so muffled them in mysticisms, fancies and falsehoods, have caricatured them into forms so inconceivable, as to shock reasonable thinkers... Happy in the prospect of a restoration of primitive Christianity, I must leave to younger persons to encounter and lop off the false branches which have been engrafted into it by the mythologists of the middle and modern ages (Jefferson's Complete Works vol. 7 pp. 210 and 257).

I believe Roger Williams described the dilemma of Christianity during the early years of America's beginning which I quoted previously:

> There is no regularly constituted church on earth, nor any person authorized to administer any church ordinance; nor can there be until new apostles are sent by the Great Head of the Church for whose coming I am seeking (Picturesque America, p. 502).

With the creation of the Constitution and men who loved God in responsible government positions, religious freedom was guaranteed and the Church of Jesus Christ could be restored in America from which the full gospel of Jesus Christ could be taken to the rest of the world. The stage was set for God to reveal his secrets to a prophet as indicated in Amos 3:7.

CHAPTER SEVENTEEN

THE RESTORATION OF THE CHURCH OF JESUS CHRIST AND HIS GOSPEL

*I*n each chapter of this book, you can find reminders of what has been lost from the gospel of Jesus Christ and of what needs to be restored. The first eleven chapters covered the "Gospel of Jesus Christ" as the original Bible Christians understood it. Chapter Twelve outlined God's "everlasting" covenant with Abraham's seed to "bless all families of the earth" with the gospel of Jesus Christ, which still needs to be fulfilled. Chapter Thirteen covered another record of scripture, the Book of Mormon, a second witness of Jesus Christ, and a record that needed to be brought forth in these latter-days. Chapter Fourteen described the Church Jesus Christ established as outlined in the New Testament. Chapter Fifteen described the apostasy (falling away) of the Church of Jesus Christ and the Reformation which followed. Great men attempted to "reform" the Catholic Church, which started numerous Protestant Churches. Chapter Sixteen detailed the importance of America as a place where God inspired the "founding fathers" to establish a Constitution granting religious freedom for those who gathered here.

If you believe there was an apostasy and that there was a need to restore what was lost then you are ready for this chapter. This chapter is the story of the restoration of both the Church of Jesus Christ and the Gospel of Jesus Christ. Many of the quotes in this chapter are from the "Doctrine and Covenants," which is a modern book of scripture and contains many of the revelations that were necessary to restore the church and the gospel of Jesus Christ back on the earth.

What was lost because of the Apostasy and needed to be restored?

- The fullness of the gospel of Jesus Christ, which is necessary for salvation.

- The Priesthood authority so men could again be "called of God" and preach the gospel of Jesus Christ.

- The same church organization, which Christ established with a foundation of Apostles and Prophets.

With the rediscovery of America, there was a place and a people prepared for the Restoration of all things. The War of Independence in 1776 and the creation of The United States Constitution in 1787 were the final events which God inspired to prepare a safe place for The Church of Jesus Christ to be restored and spread to all nations. What was needed now was a prophet of God for "surely the Lord God will do nothing, but he revealeth his secret unto his servants the prophets" (Amos 3:7).

With these things accomplished, God prepared a family in Sharon, Vermont to raise a prophet in these latter days. The names of the husband and wife were Joseph Smith, Sr. and Lucy Mack Smith. The Smiths were hard working farmers and Bible believing Christians. On December 23, 1805 God sent a son to this God-fearing family, who named the fourth of their ten children Joseph Smith, Jr.

Due to crop failures, the Smith family moved to western New York, where they purchased one hundred acres near Palmyra. The area was sparsely settled and educational opportunities were limited, perhaps that is the reason the Bible was a central part of the Smith family's life.

When Joseph Smith was fourteen years old he had a spiritual experience which changed the lives of Joseph Smith and his family. I am now going to share Joseph's own story with you:

> There was in the place where we lived an unusual excitement on the subject of religion. It commenced with the Methodists, but soon became general among all the sects in that region of country. Indeed, the whole district of country seemed affected by it, and great multitudes united themselves to the different

religious parties, which created no small stir and division amongst the people,... Some were contending for the Methodist faith, some for the Presbyterian, and some for the Baptist.

In the midst of this war of words and tumult of opinions, I often said to myself: What is to be done? Who of all these parties are right; or, are they all wrong together? If any one of them be right, which is it, and how shall I know it? While I was laboring under the extreme difficulties caused by the contests of these parties of religionists, I was one day reading the Epistle of James, first chapter and fifth verse, which reads: *If any of you lack wisdom, let him ask of God, that giveth to all men liberally, and upbraideth not; and it shall be given him.*

Never did any passage of scripture come with more power to the heart of man than this did at this time to mine. It seemed to enter with great force into every feeling of my heart. I reflected on it again and again, knowing that if any person needed wisdom from God, I did; for how to act I did not know, and unless I could get more wisdom than I then had, I would never know; for the teachers of religion of the different sects understood the same passages of scripture so differently as to destroy all confidence in settling the question by an appeal to the Bible. At length I came to the conclusion that I must either remain in darkness and confusion, or else I must do as James directs, that is, ask of God.

It was on the morning of a beautiful, clear day, early in the spring of 1820. It was the first time in my life that I had made such an attempt, for amidst all my anxieties I had never as yet made the attempt to pray vocally. After I had retired to the place where I had previously designed to go, having looked around me, and finding myself alone, I kneeled down and began to offer up the desires of my heart to God. I had scarcely done so, when immediately I was seized upon by some power which entirely overcame me, and had such an astonishing influence over me as to bind my tongue so that I could not speak. Thick darkness gathered around me, and it seemed to me for a time as if I were doomed to sudden destruction.

But, exerting all my powers to call upon God to deliver me out of the power of this enemy which had seized upon me, and at the very moment when I was ready to sink into despair and abandon myself to destruction—not to an imaginary ruin, but to the power of some actual being from the unseen world, who had such marvelous power as I had never before felt in any being—just at this moment of great alarm, I saw a pillar of light exactly over my head, above the brightness of the sun, which descended gradually until it fell upon me.

It no sooner appeared than I found myself delivered from the enemy which held me bound. When the light rested upon me I saw two Personages, whose brightness and glory defy all description, standing above me in the air. One of them spake unto me, calling me be name and said, pointing to the other—*This is My Beloved Son, Hear Him!*

My object in going to inquire of the Lord was to know which of all the sects was right, that I might know which to join. No sooner, therefore, did I get possession of myself, so as to be able to speak, than I asked the Personages who stood above me in the light, which of all the sects was right (for at this time it had never entered into my heart that all were wrong)—and which I should join. I was answered that I must join none of them, for they were all wrong; and the Personage who addressed me said that all their creeds were an abomination in His sight; that those professors were all corrupt; that: "they draw near to me with their lips, but their hearts are far from me, they teach for doctrines the commandments of men, having a form of godliness, but they deny the power thereof."

He again forbade me to join with any of them; and many other things did he say unto me, which I cannot write at this time. When I came to myself again, I found myself lying on my back, looking up into heaven (Joseph Smith History 1:5-20).

Joseph Smith was in his fifteenth year when God the Father and His Son Jesus Christ appeared to him. What did he learn from this marvelous experience? He learned that God and Christ are two separate resurrected beings, a Bible truth which contradicted the creeds of men (e.g., the Athanasian Creed which says, "God, Jesus Christ and the Holy Ghost are not three Gods but one God. And they are incomprehensible.") God knew Joseph and called him by name. He was instructed by Jesus Christ, the Son of God, and told to join no church because none of them were true.

He shared this glorious vision with one of the local ministers. Joseph Smith relates his response:

> I was greatly surprised at his (the minister's) behavior; he treated my communication not only lightly, but with great contempt, saying it was all of the devil, that there were no such things as visions or revelations in these days; that all such things had ceased with the apostles, and that there would never be any more of them (Joseph Smith History 1:21).

(It seems strange that a minister would believe that Satan still had power to do his evil work but that God and Christ appear to have retired.)

> I soon found, however, that my telling the story had excited a great deal of prejudice against me among professors of religion, and was the cause of great persecution, which continued to increase; and though I was an obscure boy, only between fourteen and fifteen years of age, and my circumstances in life such as to make a boy of no consequence in the world, yet men of high standing would take notice sufficient to excite the public mind against me, and create a bitter persecution; and this was common among all the sects–all united to persecute me.

> I have thought since, that I felt much like Paul (the apostle), when he made his defense before King Agrippa, and related the account of the vision he had when he saw a light, and heard a voice; but still there were but few who believed him; some said he was dishonest, others said he was mad; and he was ridiculed and reviled. But all this did not destroy the reality of his vision.

He had seen a vision, he knew he had, and all the persecution under heaven could not make it otherwise; and though they should persecute him unto death, yet he knew, and would know to his latest breath, that he had both seen a light and heard a voice speaking unto him, and all the world could not make him think or believe otherwise.

So it was with me. I had actually seen a light, and in the midst of that light I saw two Personages, and they did in reality speak to me; and though I was hated and persecuted for saying that I had seen a vision, yet it was true; and while they were persecuting me, reviling me, and speaking all manner of evil against me falsely for so saying, I was led to say in my heart: Why persecute me for telling the truth? I have actually seen a vision; and who am I that I can withstand God, or why does the world think to make me deny what I have actually seen? For I had seen a vision; I knew it, and I knew that God knew it, and I could not deny it, neither dared I do it; at least I knew that by so doing I would offend God, and come under condemnation.

I had now got my mind satisfied so far as the sectarian world was concerned—that it was not my duty to join with any of them, but to continue as I was until further directed. I had found the testimony of James to be true—that a man who lacked wisdom might ask of God, and obtain, and not be upbraided. (Joseph Smith History 1:22, 24-26)

It should be no surprise to the reader to find out Joseph Smith and his followers were persecuted from the day of this vision (1820). Even after Joseph Smith and his brother, Hyrum, were murdered on June 27, 1844, the persecution continued.

This personal account of Joseph Smith's prayer and the appearance of God and his Son Jesus Christ marks the beginning of the Restoration of the Gospel and The Church of Jesus Christ in these the latter days. This story may be the most difficult one you have ever been asked to believe; however, Christians in the Bible had similar experiences. We need to ask ourselves if we believe this Bible scripture: **"Surely the Lord God will do nothing, but he revealeth his secret unto his servants the prophets"** (Amos 3:7).

God is not dead. His work is not finished. This world was in need of a prophet. Joseph Smith claimed to be a prophet. A prophet of God knows he is a prophet and proclaims it regardless of disbelief and persecution. I am going to ask you to apply the scriptural test for a prophet of God that is recorded in Matthew 7:16-20. In essence it is: **"Wherefore, by their fruits ye shall know them."** In other words, we need to examine what "prophets" accomplished in their lifetime. Now we will talk about what Joseph Smith accomplished in his short 39 years on this earth.

When Joseph Smith was almost 18 years old (September 21, 1823) he prayed again for guidance and was visited by a resurrected person. This is Joseph Smith's account:

> He called me by name, and said unto me that he was a messenger sent from the presence of God to me, and that his name was Moroni; **that God had a work for me to do;** and that my name should be had for good and evil among all nations, kindreds, and tongues, or that it should be both good and evil spoken of among all people. He said there was a book deposited, written upon gold plates, giving an account of the former inhabitants of this continent, and the source from which they sprang. He also said that the fullness of the everlasting Gospel was contained in it, as delivered by the Savior to the ancient inhabitants; also, that there were two stones in silver bows—and these stones, fastened to a breast-plate, constituted what is called the Urim and Thummim—deposited with the plates; and the possession and use of these stones were what constituted "seers" in ancient or former times; and that God had prepared them for the purpose of translating the book (Joseph Smith History 1:33-35)

Moroni then quoted scriptures from the Bible. He first quoted part of the third and fourth chapters of Malachi in the Old Testament. In addition he quoted the eleventh chapter of Isaiah, saying that it was about to be fulfilled. I will quote three of the significant verses:

> And it shall come to pass in that day, that the Lord shall set his hand again the second time to recover the remnant of his people, which shall be left... And he shall set up an ensign for the nations, and shall assemble the outcasts of Israel, and gather

together the dispersed of Judah (Jews) from the four corners of the earth. The envy also of Ephraim shall depart, and the adversaries of Judah shall be cut off: Ephraim shall not envy Judah, and Judah shall not vex Ephraim" (Isaiah 11:11-13).

In a previous chapter (chapter eleven) of this book we found God's covenant with Abraham was "everlasting" and had not been fulfilled during Bible times.

Moroni appeared two more times that night and repeated everything again to Joseph Smith. He said the three visits from this glorious messenger occupied the entire night. The next day Moroni again appeared to Joseph Smith during the daytime. He again related everything he had said during the previous night. He then commanded Joseph to tell his father about this visit. Joseph shared what he had learned with his father. His father believed him and told Joseph it was from God and to do as the messenger commanded. Joseph then went to the Hill Cumorah where the gold plates of the Book of Mormon were buried. (The Hill Cumorah is about four miles from Palmyra, N.Y.) Joseph gives this account of seeing the historical record for the first time:

I made an attempt to take them out, but was forbidden by the messenger, and was again informed that the time for bringing them forth had not yet arrived, neither would it, until four years from that time; but he told me that I should come to that place precisely in one year from that time, and that he would there meet with me, and that I should continue to do so until the time should come for obtaining the plates.

Accordingly, as I had been commanded, I went at the end of each year, and at each time I found the same messenger there, and received instruction and intelligence from him at each of our interviews, respecting what the Lord was going to do, and how and in what manner his kingdom was to be conducted in the last days.

At length the time arrived for obtaining the plates, the Urim and Thummim, and the breastplate. On the 22nd day of September, 1827, having gone as usual at the end of another year to the place where they were deposited, the same heavenly messenger delivered them up to me with this charge: that I should be responsible for them; that if I should let them go carelessly, or through any neglect of mine, I should be cut off; but that if I would use all my endeavors to preserve them, until he, the messenger, should call for them, they should be protected (Joseph Smith History 1:53-54, 59).

Joseph Smith, who was married on January 18, 1827, already had the responsibility of earning a living and now had the responsibility of translating and protecting this sacred record. The Lord sent him a young school teacher, Oliver Cowdery, to act as a scribe while Joseph did the translating. During this process, they found accounts of baptism for the remission of sins. Since there was much disagreement about baptism, they took the matter to the Lord. On May 15, 1829, Joseph and Oliver went into the woods to pray. A heavenly messenger appeared to them and said he was John the Baptist, the person who had baptized Jesus Christ. He said he was sent to confer the Aaronic Priesthood upon them. He put his hands on their heads and said:

Upon you my fellow servants, in the name of Messiah I confer the Priesthood of Aaron, which holds the keys of the ministering of angels, and of the gospel of repentance, and of baptism by immersion for the remission of sins; and this shall never be taken again from the earth, until the sons of Levi do offer again an offering unto the Lord in righteousness (Doctrine and Covenants, section 13).

In August of 1830 Joseph Smith the prophet received this revelation:

Listen to the voice of Jesus Christ, your Lord, your God, and your Redeemer, whose word is quick and powerful. ...Which John (John the Baptist) I have sent unto you, my servants, Joseph Smith, Jun., and Oliver Cowdery, to ordain you unto the first priesthood which you have received, that you might be called and ordained even as Aaron (Doctrine and Covenants 27:1, 8).

Aaron was the brother of the Prophet Moses. Aaron was given the lesser priesthood, which is called the Aaronic Priesthood. The Apostle Paul said: **"And no man taketh this honour (Priesthood)**

unto himself, but he that is called of God, as was Aaron" (Hebrews 5:4). Men are "called of God" to hold the Priesthood of God in a consistent manner. In both the Old and New Testaments the calling came through Prophets. **"Surely the Lord GOD will do nothing, but he revealeth his secret unto his servants the prophets"** (Amos 3:7).

The Restoration of the Church of Jesus Christ and the Gospel of Jesus Christ came through prophets as well. Jesus Christ is the head of his church and he does the choosing. To restore his church, Jesus Christ sent those who had been chosen by him and "called of God" in previous dispensations to restore the authority they held to the prophet of this dispensation. [If the reader is hesitant about accepting the return of ancient prophets who were resurrected, then it may help to read this scripture in the New Testament: **"And the graves were opened; and many bodies of the saints which slept arose, And came out of the graves after his resurrection, and went into the holy city, and appeared unto many"** (Matthew 27:52-53). Righteous men of God who have died have been resurrected so that they can assist in the restoration of the Church of Jesus Christ.]

In 1829 Joseph Smith and Oliver Cowdery received the Melchizedek Priesthood and were ordained as apostles under the hands of Peter, James and John, apostles who were called and ordained by Christ during Bible times:

> **And also with Peter, and James, and John, whom I have sent unto you, by whom I have ordained you and confirmed you to be apostles, and especial witnesses of my name, and bear the keys of your ministry and of the same things which I revealed unto them; Unto whom I have committed the keys of my kingdom, and a dispensation of the gospel for the last times; and for the fullness of times, in the which I will gather together in one all things, both which are in heaven, and which are on earth;** (Doctrine and Covenants 27:12-13).

In June of 1829 the translation of The Book of Mormon was completed and three special witnesses of this record were provided by the Lord. Oliver Cowdery, David Whitmer, and Martin Harris were shown the golden plates by an angel from

God and they heard a voice saying: **"These plates have been revealed by the power of God, and they have been translated by the power of God. The translation of them which you have seen is correct, and I command you to bear record of what you now see and hear"** (History of the Church, Joseph Smith, Vol 1 p54).

They never denied this testimony. (The testimony of the Three Witnesses is in Appendix 5.) There were eight other witnesses who also saw the plates from which The Book of Mormon was translated.

On April 6, 1830 in the state of New York, Joseph Smith and five other men formally organized the restored Church of Jesus Christ. The Church of Jesus Christ of Latter-day Saints now numbers over fourteen million (in 2012) which is a remarkable achievement for a church with an unpaid ministry and missionary force which is without equal in the world.

In 1833 the Prophet Joseph Smith received a revelation called the "Word of Wisdom." This is the basis for the counsel against the use of tobacco, liquor, coffee and tea.

In 1835, Twelve Apostles were called as special witnesses of the Lord Jesus Christ. "The twelve traveling councilors are called to be the Twelve Apostles, or special witnesses of the name of Christ in all the world–thus differing from other officers in the church in the duties of their calling… The Twelve being sent out, holding the keys, to open the door by the proclamation of the gospel of Jesus Christ, and first unto the Gentiles and then unto the Jews" (Doctrine and Covenants 107:23, 35).

In July 1835, Joseph Smith translated The Book of Abraham from papyrus scrolls, which were purchased from a Michael Chandler, who was exhibiting them. The Book of Abraham contains writings of the ancient prophet Abraham in the Old Testament. I include only a few verses to show the significance of this book of scripture:

> My name is Jehovah, and I know the end from the beginning; therefore my hand shall be over thee. And I will make of thee a great nation, and I will bless thee above measure, and make thy name great among all nations, and thou shalt be a blessing unto thy seed after thee, **that in their hands they shall bear this ministry and Priesthood unto all nations;**

And I will bless them through thy name; **for as many as receive this Gospel** shall be called after thy name, and shall be accounted thy seed, and shall rise up and bless thee, as their father;

And I will bless them that bless thee, and curse them that curse thee; and in thee and in thy seed, for I give unto thee a promise that this right shall continue in thee, and in thy seed after thee...shall all the families of the earth be blessed, **even with the blessings of the Gospel, which are the blessings of salvation, even of life eternal"** (The Book of Abraham 2:8-11). (I have emphasized in bold that which is missing from Genesis 12:1-3.)

On March 27, 1836 a temple or "House of the Lord" was dedicated in Kirtland, Ohio. Temples and temple ordinances have always been an important part of Christianity. It is not a church meetinghouse. "A temple is literally a house of the Lord, a holy sanctuary in which sacred ceremonies and ordinances of the gospel are performed by and for the living and also in behalf of the dead. A place where the Lord may come, it is the most holy of any place of worship on the earth" (Bible Dictionary, King James Version, published by The Church of Jesus Christ of Latter-day Saints).

The Savior appeared in the Kirtland temple:

We saw the Lord standing upon the breastwork of the pulpit, before us; ...his voice was as the sound of the rushing of great waters, even the voice of Jehovah, saying: I am the first and the last; I am he who liveth, I am he who was slain; I am your advocate with the Father....For behold, I have accepted this house, and my name shall be here; and I will manifest myself to my people in mercy in this house" (Doctrine and Covenants 110:2, 3, 7).

After this vision closed, the heavens were again opened unto us; and Moses appeared before us, and committed unto us the keys of the gathering of Israel from the four parts of the earth, and the leading of the ten tribes from the land of the north (Doctrine and Covenants 110:11).

After this, Elias appeared, and committed the dispensation of the gospel of Abraham, saying that in us and our seed all generations after us should be blessed (Doctrine and Covenants 110:12).

After this vision had closed, another great and glorious vision burst upon us; for Elijah the prophet, who was taken to heaven without tasting death, stood before us, and said: Behold, the time has fully come, which was spoken of by the mouth of Malachi—testifying that he [Elijah] should be sent, before the great and dreadful day of the Lord come—To turn the hearts of the fathers to the children, and the children to the fathers, lest the whole earth be smitten with a curse—Therefore, the keys of this dispensation are committed into your hands; and by this ye may know that the great and dreadful day of the Lord is near, even at the doors (Doctrine and Covenants 110:13-16).

Joseph Smith, the prophet, said:

It is sufficient to know, in this case, that the earth will be smitten with a curse unless there is a welding link of some kind or other between the fathers and the children, upon some subject or other—and behold what is that subject? It is the baptism for the dead. For we without them cannot be made perfect; neither can they without us be made perfect. Neither can they nor we be made perfect without those who have died in the gospel also; for it is necessary in the ushering of the dispensation of the fullness of times, which dispensation is now beginning to usher in,... (Doctrine and Covenants 128:18).

This revelation, we believe, has had a profound effect upon all people to search out the records of their deceased ancestors. The Church of Jesus Christ of Latter-day Saints has the greatest genealogy library in the world. If you want help finding your ancestors, you are welcome to visit a "Family History Center" which may be in one of our churches in your area.

And now, my dearly beloved brethren and sisters, let me assure you that these are principles in relation to the dead and the living that cannot be lightly passed over, as pertaining to our salvation. For their salvation is necessary and essential to our salvation, as Paul says concerning the fathers—that they without us cannot be made perfect—neither can we without our dead be made perfect (Doctrine and Covenants 128:15) (Hebrews 11:40).

After being organized with a quorum of twelve apostles and having received divine authority to act in God's name, the restored

Church of Jesus Christ was now ready to fulfill its purpose, and missionaries were called to spread the restored gospel of Jesus Christ in all the world. Missionaries were sent to Canada and their success there soon led to very successful missionary work in Great Britain.

As the church grew so did the persecution and adversity. This opposition caused the Church to move westward from Ohio to Missouri. The opposition and persecution came to a head in Missouri. The members of the Church numbered between 12,000 and 15,000 in the state in 1838. Mobs formed to persecute the members and when members tried to defend themselves they were falsely accused of causing the contention.

Governor Boggs of Missouri created a state militia of over 2,000 men and issued an "Extermination Order" against the Mormons. They were to drive 12,000 defenseless citizens from the state in the dead of winter. In part the order said: "The Mormons must be treated as enemies and must be exterminated or driven from the state, if necessary for the public good." After the Mormons were driven out, all of their property was either destroyed or stolen by their enemies.

In the appeal to Congress and the President of the United States in 1839, the amount of their losses was estimated at two million dollars. In addition to their property losses, the Prophet Joseph Smith paid lawyer's fees for the defense of the people and himself of about fifty thousand dollars, with little to show for it. Joseph Smith and several of his companions were arrested for treason and other ridiculous charges, and were put in "Liberty Jail," Liberty, Missouri for six months.

While in jail the Prophet Joseph Smith pled with the Lord for the members of the church, "Remember thy suffering saints, O our God; and thy servants will rejoice in thy name forever" (Doctrine and Covenants, Section 121:6).

He received some marvelous revelations that have given comfort and perspective for all those who have been unlawfully persecuted. I will extract some of the divine counsel because it may be valuable as we prepare for the difficult times preceding the "Second Coming of the Lord."

> My son, peace be unto thy soul; thine adversity and thine afflictions shall be but a small moment; And then, if thou endure it well, God shall exalt thee on high; thou shall triumph over all thy foes. Thy friends do stand by thee, and they shall

hail thee again with warm hearts and friendly hands. Thou art not yet as Job; thy friends do not contend against thee, neither charge thee with transgression, as they did Job.

For there is a time appointed for every man, according as his works shall be. God shall give unto you knowledge by his Holy Spirit, yea, by the unspeakable gift of the Holy Ghost, that has not been revealed since the world was until now; (Doctrine and Covenants 121:7-10, 25-26).

The ends of the earth shall inquire after thy name, and fools shall have thee in derision, and hell shall rage against thee; While the pure in heart, and the wise, and the noble, and the virtuous, shall seek counsel, and authority, and blessings constantly from under thy hand.

And thy people shall never be turned against thee by the testimony of traitors.

And if thou shouldst be cast into the pit, or into the hands of murderers, and the sentence of death passed upon thee; if thou be cast into the deep; if the billowing surge conspire against thee; if fierce winds become thine enemy; if the heavens gather blackness, and all the elements combine to hedge up the way; and above all, if the very jaws of hell shall gape open the mouth wide after thee, know thou, my son, **that all these things shall give thee experience, and shall be for thy good.**

The Son of Man hath descended below them all. Art thou greater than he? Therefore, hold on thy way, and the priesthood shall remain with thee; for their bounds are set, they cannot pass. Thy days are known, and thy years shall not be numbered less; therefore, fear not what man can do, for God shall be with you forever and ever (Doctrine and Covenants 122:1-3, 7-9).

And also it is an imperative duty that we owe to all the rising generation, and to all the pure in heart—For there are many yet on the earth among all sects, parties, and denominations, who are blinded by the subtle craftiness of men, whereby they lie in wait to deceive, and who are only kept from the truth because they know not where to find it—

Therefore, that we should waste and wear out our lives in bringing to light all the hidden things of darkness, wherein we know them; and they are truly manifest from heaven— These should then be attended to with great earnestness.

Therefore, dearly beloved brethren, let us cheerfully do all things that lie in our power; and then may we stand still, with the utmost assurance, to see the salvation of God, and for his arm to be revealed (Doctrine and Covenants 123:11-14, 17).

The Mormons were driven out of the state of Missouri in the winter of 1838-1839. They went to the state of Illinois where they were made welcome. They purchased and drained swampland on the Mississippi River and created the city of Nauvoo. Within five years Nauvoo became the largest and most beautiful city in the state of Illinois. There were twenty thousand members of the church in and around Nauvoo. This growth came from successful missionary work in Great Britain, Canada and the United States. Now the Mormons had a political presence, which was feared because they had the balance of power in an election. The persecution the Mormons had in Missouri was now mounting in Illinois. The Governor of the State of Missouri (Thomas Reynolds) issued new indictments against Joseph Smith based on old charges and sent them to the Governor of Illinois, Thomas Ford. Governor Ford issued a warrant for the arrest of Joseph Smith. Joseph Smith and other leaders surrendered themselves and were imprisoned in Carthage Jail.

"When Joseph went to Carthage to deliver himself up to the pretended requirements of the law, two or three days previous to his assassination, he said: 'I am going like a lamb to the slaughter; but I am calm as a summer's morning; I have a conscience void of offense toward God, and towards all men. I SHALL DIE INNOCENT, AND IT SHALL BE YET SAID OF ME—HE WAS MURDERED IN COLD BLOOD' " (Doctrine and Covenants 135:4).

On June 27, 1844 a mob of about 150 to 200 men broke into Carthage Jail and murdered the Prophet Joseph Smith and his brother Hyrum. This was not the end of the persecution for these people who had been driven out of Ohio and Missouri without protection from the government of the United States. The Prophet Joseph Smith had forewarned the members earlier that month:

It is thought by some that our enemies would be satisfied by my destruction, but I tell you as soon as they have shed my blood, they will thirst for the blood of every man in whose heart dwells a single spark of the spirit of the fullness of the Gospel. The opposition of these men is moved by the spirit of the adversary of all righteousness. It is not only to destroy me, but every man and woman who dares believe the doctrine that God hath inspired me to teach to this generation (Essentials of Church History, (p.305).

On September 22, 1845, a mass meeting was held in Quincy, Illinois to take action against the members of the Church. Following the meeting the Quincy Whig (newspaper) made this statement in this boasted land of liberty:

It is a settled thing that the public sentiment of the State is against the 'Mormons,' and it will be in vain for them to contend against it; and to prevent bloodshed, and the sacrifice of many lives on both sides, it is their duty to obey the public will and leave the State as speedily as possible. That they will do this we have confident hope and that too, before the next extreme is resorted to—that of force" (Essentials of Church History, p. 326).

So the Mormons left the United States and went out west, because "Freedom of Religion in America" at that time was "an empty promise for the Mormons." In 1842 the Prophet Joseph Smith prophesied the Saints would continue to suffer much affliction and "some of you will live to go and assist in making settlements and build cities and see the Saints become a mighty people in the midst of the Rocky Mountains." (History of the Church 7:567)

The Mormons were again forced to leave their homes and the exodus from Nauvoo, Illinois began in 1846. "Leaving Nauvoo was an act of faith for the Saints. They departed without knowing exactly where they were going or when they would arrive at a place to settle. They only knew they were on the verge of being driven out of Illinois by their enemies and their leaders had received revelation to locate a refuge somewhere in the Rocky Mountains" Their new home would be outside of the United States (a part of "upper California" administered by Mexico). (Church History in the Fullness of Times" p. 309, 310)

Brigham Young and the other apostles planned this monumental migration of over 12,000 people across 1,300 miles of uncharted wilderness. By 1869 more than 68,000 Mormon pioneers made this trek, mostly with ox-drawn wagons, but some with only handcarts. The first group of pioneers arrived in the barren Salt Lake Valley, a place no one else wanted, on July 24, 1847. Despite the desolate and uninviting conditions, the Church thrived in this new gathering place. Missionaries were sent to all parts of the world and today the church numbers about 14 million Bible Christians, with over one half of them living outside of the United States.

Earlier, I stated that one of the evidences of a prophet is: A prophet knows he is a prophet and claims to be a prophet of God regardless of ridicule and persecution. Joseph Smith was the prophet of "The Restoration." Many prophets gave their lives because they were prophets. Joseph Smith gave his life for the restored gospel of Jesus Christ. John Taylor, another latter day prophet said:

> Joseph Smith, the Prophet and Seer of the Lord, has done more, save Jesus only, for the salvation of men in this world, than any other man that ever lived in it. In the short space of twenty years, he has brought forth the Book of Mormon, which he translated by the gift and power of God, and has been the means of publishing it on two continents; has sent the fulness of the everlasting gospel, which it contained, to the four quarters of the earth; has brought forth the revelations and commandments which compose this book of Doctrine and Covenants, and many other wise documents and instructions for the benefit of the children of men; gathered many thousands of the Later-day Saints; founded a great city,

and left a fame and name that cannot be slain. He lived great, and he died great in the eyes of God and his people; and like most the Lord's anointed in ancient times, has sealed his mission and his works with his own blood; and so has his brother Hyrum. In life they were not divided, and in death they were not separated! (Doctrine and Covenants 135:3).

After meeting the prophet Joseph Smith, Josiah Quincy, a former mayor of Boston, wrote the following:

It is by no means improbable that some future textbook, for the use of generations yet unborn, will contain a question something like this: What historical American of the nineteenth century has exerted the most powerful influence upon the destinies of his countrymen? And it is by no means impossible that the answer to that interrogatory may be thus written: *Joseph Smith, the Mormon prophet.* And the reply, absurd as it doubtless seems to most men now living, may be an obvious commonplace to their descendants. History deals in surprises and paradoxes quite as startling as this.

The man who established a religion in this age of free debate, who was and is to-day accepted by hundreds of thousands as a direct emissary from the Most High, –such a rare human being is not to be disposed of by pelting his memory with unsavory epithets (Josiah Quincy, Figures of the Past, Boston: Little, Brown and Co., 1883, p 376).

Here is the Bible standard or test for a Prophet of God: "Ye shall know them by their fruits" (Matthew 7:16). With that in mind please consider this memorial tribute to the Prophet Joseph Smith:

Here is a man who was born in the stark hills of Vermont; who was reared in the back woods of New York; who never looked inside a college or high school; who lived in six States, no one of which would own him during his lifetime; who spent months in the vile prisons of the period; who, even when he had his freedom, was hounded like a fugitive; who was covered once with a coat of tar and feathers, and left for dead; who, with his following, was driven by irate neighbors from New York to Ohio, from Ohio to Missouri, and from Missouri to Illinois; and who, at the unripe age of thirty-eight, was shot to death by a mob with painted faces.

Yet this man became mayor of the biggest town in Illinois (Nauvoo) and the state's most prominent citizen, the commander of the largest body of trained soldiers in the nation outside the Federal army, the founder of cities and of a university, and aspired to become President of the United States.

He wrote a book (The Book of Mormon) which has baffled the literary critics for a hundred years (182 years now) and which is today more widely read than any other volume save the Bible. On the threshold of an organizing age he established the most nearly perfect social mechanism in the modern world, and developed a religious philosophy that challenges anything of the kind in history, for completeness and cohesion. And he set up the machinery for an economic system that would take the brood of Fears out of the heart of man—the fear of want through sickness, old age, unemployment, and poverty.

In thirty nations (160 nations today) are men and women who look upon him as a greater leader than Moses and a greater prophet than Isaiah; his disciples now number close to a million (14 million today); and already a granite shaft pierces the sky over the place where he was born, and another over the place where he is credited with having received the inspiration for his Book (Joseph Smith the American Prophet by John Henry Evans).

I now add my own testimony. **Joseph Smith is a prophet of God**. He provided more scripture than any other prophet, almost equal to all other prophets put together. Once you have read the scriptures he translated and revelations he received, you will know it was impossible for anyone to have written all of this on his own. If your testimony of Jesus Christ came from study of the scriptures, sincere prayer, and living by his teachings; then I ask you to read The Book of Mormon, which is another witness of Jesus Christ. Then ask your Heavenly Father if it is true. "If ye shall ask with a sincere heart, with real intent, having faith in Christ, he will manifest the truth of it unto you by the power of the Holy Ghost. And by the power of the Holy Ghost ye may know the truth of all things" (Book of Mormon, Moroni 10:4-5).

Joseph Smith was once asked the question: "What are the fundamental principles of your religion?"

He replied, "The fundamental principles of our religion are the testimony of the Apostles and Prophets, concerning Jesus Christ, that He died, was buried, and rose again the third day, and ascended into heaven; and all other things which pertain to our religion are only appendages to it" (Teachings of Presidents of the Church: Joseph Smith (2007 p49) (Aug 2012 Ensign p49).

I believe this statement by the Prophet Joseph Smith answered the question of whether Mormons are Bible Christians.

Here is the testimony of modern Apostles of The Church of Jesus Christ of Latter-day Saints published January 1, 2000:

The Living Christ

As we commemorate the birth of Jesus Christ two millennia ago, we offer our testimony of the reality of His matchless life and the infinite virtue of His great atoning sacrifice. None other has had so profound an influence upon all who have lived and will yet live upon the earth.

He was the Great Jehovah of the Old Testament, the Messiah of the New. Under the direction of His Father, He was the creator of the earth. "All things were made by him; and without him was not any thing made that was made" (John 1:3). Though sinless, He was baptized to fulfill all righteousness. He "went about doing good" (Acts 10:38), yet was despised for it. His gospel was a message of peace and goodwill. He entreated all to follow His example. He walked the roads of Palestine, healing the sick, causing the blind to see, and raising the dead. He taught the truths of eternity, the reality of our premortal existence, the purpose of our life on earth, and the potential for the sons and daughters of God in the life to come.

He instituted the sacrament as a reminder of His great atoning sacrifice. He was arrested and condemned on spurious charges, convicted to satisfy a mob, and sentenced to die on Calvary's cross. He gave His life to atone for the sins of all mankind. His was a great vicarious gift in behalf of all who would ever live upon the earth.

We solemnly testify that His life, which is central to all human history, neither began in Bethlehem nor concluded on Calvary. He was the Firstborn of the Father, the Only Begotten Son in the flesh, the Redeemer of the world.

He rose from the grave to "become the firstfruits of them that slept" (1 Corinthians 15:20). As Risen Lord, He visited among those He had loved in life. He also ministered among His "other sheep" (John 10:16) in ancient America. In the modern world, He and His Father appeared to the boy Joseph Smith, ushering in the long-promised "dispensation of the fullness of times" (Ephesians 1:10).

Of the Living Christ, the Prophet Joseph wrote: "His eyes were as a flame of fire; the hair of his head was white like the pure snow; his countenance shone above the brightness of the sun; and his voice was as the sound of the rushing of great waters, even the voice of Jehovah, saying:

"I am the first and the last; I am he who liveth, I am he who was slain; I am your advocate with the Father (D&C 110:3-4).

Of Him the Prophet also declared: "And now, after the many testimonies which have been given of him, this is the testimony, last of all, which we give of him: That he lives!

"For we saw him, even on the right hand of God; and we heard the voice bearing record that he is the Only Begotten of the Father–

"That by him, and through him, and of him, the worlds are and were created, and the inhabitants thereof are begotten sons and daughters unto God" (D&C 76:22-24).

We declare in words of solemnity that His priesthood and His Church have been restored upon the earth–"built upon the foundation of ...apostles and prophets, Jesus Christ himself being the chief corner stone" (Ephesians 2:20).

We testify that He will someday return to earth. "And the glory of the Lord shall be revealed, and all flesh shall see it together" (Isaiah 40:5). He will rule as King of Kings and reign as Lord of Lords, and every knee shall bend and every tongue shall speak in worship before Him. Each of us will stand to be judged of Him according to our works and the desires of our hearts.

We bear testimony, as His duly ordained Apostles–that Jesus in the Living Christ, the immortal Son of God. He is the great King Immanuel, who stands today on the right hand of His Father. He is the light, the life, and the hope of the world. His way is the path that leads to happiness in this life and eternal life in the world to come. God be thanked for the matchless gift of His divine Son. (Signed by the First Presidency and the Quorum of the Twelve Apostles)

The Articles of Faith

In 1842 the Prophet Joseph Smith wrote the following thirteen "Articles of Faith" of The Church of Jesus Christ of Latter-day Saints. They form a simple declaration of many doctrines of the Church:

1. We believe in God, the Eternal Father, and in His Son, Jesus Christ, and in the Holy Ghost.

2. We believe that men will be punished for their own sins, and not for Adam's transgression.

3. We believe that through the Atonement of Christ, all mankind may be saved, by obedience to the laws and ordinances of the Gospel.

4. We believe that the first principles and ordinances of the Gospel are: first, Faith in the Lord Jesus Christ; second, Repentance; third, Baptism by immersion for the remission of sins; fourth, Laying on of hands for the gift of the Holy Ghost.

5. We believe that a man must be called of God, by prophecy, and by the laying on of hands by those who are in authority, to preach the Gospel and administer in the ordinances thereof.

6. We believe in the same organization that existed in the Primitive Church, namely, apostles, prophets, pastors, teachers, evangelists, and so forth.

7. We believe in the gift of tongues, prophecy, revelation, visions, healing, interpretation of tongues, and so forth.

8. We believe the Bible to be the word of God as far as it is translated correctly; we also believe the Book of Mormon to be the word of God.

9. We believe all that God has revealed, all that He does now reveal and we believe that He will yet reveal many great and important things pertaining to the Kingdom of God.

10. We believe in the literal gathering of Israel and in the restoration of the Ten Tribes; that Zion (the New Jerusalem) will be built upon the American continent; that Christ will reign personally upon the earth; and, that the earth will be renewed and receive its paradisiacal glory.

11. We claim the privilege of worshiping Almighty God according to the dictates of our own conscience, and allow all men the same privilege, let them worship how, where, or what they may.

12. We believe in being subject to kings, presidents, rulers, and magistrates, in obeying, honoring, and sustaining the law.

13. We believe in being honest, true, chaste, benevolent, virtuous, and in doing good to all men; indeed, we may say that we follow the admonition of Paul–We believe all things, we hope all things, we have endured many things, and hope to be able to endure all things. If there be anything virtuous, lovely, or of good report or praiseworthy, we seek after these things. Joseph Smith

As this book comes to a close, I would like to pay tribute to my wife Norma. She was not raised in The Church of Jesus Christ of Latter-day Saints. She is what we call "a convert." Norma's conversion has had a powerful effect on our family of 10 children. They have all been married in the Temple for time and eternity and are active in the church. When this life is over, I believe we will realize the great work and sacrifice that mothers have had in the salvation of Heavenly Father's children. Norma had the privilege of being a "stay-at-home mom" and she has excelled in that divine role, which all of our children will acknowledge. A modern prophet said: "The most important work you and I will ever do will be within the walls of our own homes" (President Harold B. Lee). My wife and I believe that is true because the "foundation" of our home has always been Jesus Christ and his gospel.

It is with great admiration I now add Norma's testimony:

"It has been many years since I was introduced to The Church of Jesus Christ of Latter-day Saints. I must admit my interest was piqued by my interest in a handsome young man named H. Kay Pugmire. My interest in Kay became secondary as I was introduced to the gospel of Jesus Christ in a Sunday school class I attended before Kay left on his mission in 1952. The feelings I felt during that first Sunday school class plus what I was being taught encouraged me to want to know more. The Sunday school lesson was on the Plan of Salvation or sometimes called the Plan of Happiness and thus began my journey to learn more. When missionaries came to Bainbridge Island, where I lived with my family, I let it be known I would like them to come and teach me. Thus began a series of weekly meetings where I was taught the gospel which ended with my baptism in 1952. Not only did I join the church, but my two sisters followed and eventually our mother.

We discovered the truth, as so many others have done, because we asked God the Eternal Father, in the name of Christ, if these things were true, and when we asked with a sincere heart, with real intent, having faith in Christ, the truth was manifested to us by the power of the Holy Ghost. It has been a wonderful journey as a member of The Church of Jesus Christ of Latter-day Saints and those feelings first felt in that Sunday school class are still there. It is true! What is so wonderful is anyone can know for themselves by asking God if it is true as I did as well as my sisters and mother. The blessings are incredible when the teachings of Jesus Christ are followed.

If there is one thing that I have learned during this journey called life, it is that choices are incredibly important. I don't know all of the choices I made in my pre-mortal life, (before birth) but I do know one choice I made; it was to follow Heavenly Father's plan to be carried out by Jesus Christ. All of us born on this earth, made that same choice."

I thought it was appropriate for my wife to include her testimony at the conclusion of this book. Norma is the perfect example of a "Bible Christian." We believe our Heavenly Father brought us together so we could raise some of His children in the restored Gospel of Jesus Christ. Jesus Christ is our Savior and Redeemer. He is the way back to our Father in Heaven. It is our mission to teach our children and anyone who will listen, the simple truths of the gospel of Jesus Christ. My book has been written for this purpose.

It is my sincere hope that you now know Mormons believe that Jesus Christ should be the center of every family. The First Presidency and the Quorum of the Twelve Apostles of The Church of Jesus Christ of Latter-day Saints have issued a Proclamation to the World about the sacredness of the family. (See Appendix 6)

I feel a sacred obligation has been fulfilled in sharing my beliefs with you because you are my brothers and sisters. If after reading this book, you become a stronger "Bible Christian," bringing more blessings into the life of your family, then it has been worthwhile. May God be with you until we meet again.

CONCLUSION

*T*his book has been far more difficult to write than I anticipated. Some of the chapters came easily, which may have been due to the subject matter or to my state of mind at the time. I wonder if I have said everything that needs to be said and if I have said it clearly. I wonder if I have said too much. It is hard to write as if you were having a conversation, because you don't know if the reader would like to know just a little more.

I have been asked who my "audience" is. In other words, who am I writing to? My answer to that question changed as I wrote. Initially I was writing to those other Christians who thought Mormons were not Christians. As the book progressed I perceived my "audience-readers" as anyone who wanted the answers to the important questions of life: Who am I? Where did I come from? What is my relationship to God? What is the purpose of life? Why must I believe in Jesus Christ? Is Jesus Christ the Savior of everyone who has lived on the earth? Who is the Holy Ghost? Why do I need the Holy Ghost? Is there life after death? Will Christ come again? Will there be a Judgment Day? What happens after the Judgment?

I hope I have answered all of these questions and more. Were we to have a personal visit, I might have answered them differently. I believe that ultimately, the answers would have been the same, but the process of getting to them would have been different. I believe that every teaching situation is different because the people we teach are different. During a personal visit, I would have had time to find out about you and hopefully determine what you were ready for and needed to learn. I believe the Holy Ghost would have helped me know those things that both of us needed to learn. This book did not give me that privilege or opportunity, and I sadly missed it. I also missed the awe and the "ahas" as new friends discovered the great truths in the scriptures. I know from past experience the joy of teaching someone things I had never thought of before, because the

Holy Ghost taught me what to say. The ideal teaching situation is when the student sincerely wants to learn and the teacher allows the Holy Ghost to do the teaching. I have shared some chapters of this book with people I have met, in order to get to know some readers personally before the book was published. Their comments have influenced my writing and I want to thank them for their interest and support. They, along with many people whom I have taught in the past, have made this book possible. All of these people have become my friends and the experience of sharing these truths with them has emphasized the importance of what Jesus Christ called the Two Great Commandments: "Thou shalt love the Lord thy God with all thy heart, and with all thy soul, and with all thy mind. This is the first and great commandment. And the second is like unto it, thou shalt love thy neighbour as thyself. On these two commandments hang all the law and the prophets" (Matthew 22:37-40). You cannot live one of these commandments without the other.

Now for some final thoughts, which I hope you will ponder. Our earth life is only a day in eternity, but it is a crucial one. This is the day for which we were sent to prepare to meet God. Eternity will be a very long time to contemplate what we should have done during our short stay in mortality. It is never too late to become what we should have been. "Whatever principle of intelligence we attain unto in this life, it will rise with us in the resurrection. And if a person gains more knowledge and intelligence in this life through his diligence and obedience than another, he will have so much the advantage in the world to come" (Doctrine and Covenants 130:18-19). Do not underestimate your potential and your destiny. You are a literal child of a loving Heavenly Father and He wants you to come back to Him. Jesus Christ is the way back. "For God so loved the world, that he gave his only begotten Son, that whosoever believeth in him should not perish, but have everlasting life" (John 3:16). I sincerely pray that each of us will make that our goal.

APPENDIX 1

MY LIST OF THE SIGNS OF THE TIMES

<u>**Wars** –</u>

Iraq War: from March 2003 to December 2011. As of August 2010 the projected cost was $900 billion and 4,415 U.S. military personnel killed in action. Over 100,000 Iraqi civilians were estimated to be killed (From Wikipedia, the free encyclopedia). "The wars in Iraq and Afghanistan will ultimately cost between $4 trillion and $6 trillion, with medical care and disability benefits....the bill to taxpayers so far has been $2 trillion, plus $260 billion in interest on the resulting debt. (The Seattle Times, March 31, 2013)

Afghanistan: This is the war that President Obama called a "war of necessity," a conflict thrust upon America by the 9/11 attacks. After 11 years, the insurgents remain undefeated, corruption runs rife, and the fledgling peace process is stuck in the sand." NATO is scheduled to leave in 2014, and will "require no less than $4.1 billion a year from foreign coffers at a time when most of the countries are struggling with deficits and the specter of recession and bank failures. Without big handouts, Afghanistan can't pay for its own defense (Associated Press, May 20, 2012).

Syria: After 40 years of dictatorship a civil war has killed more than 36,000 since March 2011. "Up to 11,000 people flee Syria in 24-hour period." This brings the total registered with the UN refugee agency to 408,000 (Associated Press. Nov. 10, 2012).

Libya: The Libyan civil war, also referred to as the Libyan revolution. The war was preceded by protests in Benghazi on 15 February 2011, which led to clashes with security forces that fired on the crowd. On 16 September 2011, the National Transitional Council was recognized by the United Nations as the legal representative of Libya, replacing the Gaddafi government. On 11 September 2012 U.S. Ambassador J. Christopher Stevens was murdered with 3 other members of embassy staff (from Wikipedia).

Rumors of Wars –

Iran: Nuclear program is a threat to peace in the Middle East and to Israel's existence.

Israel: Israel confronted fire along two of its borders Sunday, with rockets landing from Gaza and a mortar shell crashing in from Syria, prompting Israel to respond with what its military described as "warning shots" at a Syrian position across the frontier for the first time in 39 years. "The world needs to understand that Israel will not sit idly by in the face of attempts to attack us." (response of Benjamin Netanyahu, Prime Minister of Israel) (The Seattle Times, November 12, 2012). **(There are specific prophecies about attacks on Israel before the second coming.)**

Egypt: After a "peaceful revolution" in February 2011 they have their first democratically elected President–Mohamed Morse. Egypt is the most populous country in the Arab world, and its revolution was the capstone event of the "Arab Spring," inspiring demonstrators in Libya, Syria and elsewhere (from Wikipedia).

China and Tibet: For at least 1500 years, the nation of Tibet has had a complex relationship with its large and powerful neighbor to the east, China. Indeed, as with China's relations with the Mongols and the Japanese, the balance of power between China and Tibet has shifted back and forth over the centuries.

China and Taiwan: Civil war 1999. Taiwan is the first multiparty democracy in more than 5,000 years of Chinese history. Mainland China believes Taiwan is a "wayward" province.

China/Japan: Senkaku Islands dispute threatens trade routes, Asian economy.

North Korea/South Korea: North Korea is the last Stalinist state on earth, and in 2006 it became the latest country to join the nuclear club. Over the past two decades, it has swung between confrontation and inch-by-inch conciliation with South Korea, its neighbor, and the United States. They are on track to develop a nuclear warhead that could hit the United States within a few years. By October 2012, North Korea claimed to have missiles that can reach the American mainland (The New York Times.com).

Worldwide Terrorism –

On September 11, 2001 terrorists hijacked four commercial jet planes and flew three of them into the World Trade Center in New York City and the Pentagon in Washington D. C. 2,749 died in New York City, 189 were killed at the Pentagon. What is the ongoing cost of Homeland Security in the U. S? Where in the world is anyone safe from terrorists?

Earthquakes (and other Natural Disasters) in Divers Places

Japan: March 2011 an 8.9 earthquake & tsunami created a nuclear crisis. 5th largest earthquake in the world since 1900. 8,000 times stronger than in New Zealand. Estimates for insurers - $50 billion.

New Zealand: The 7.0 earthquake on February 2011 was the largest to strike that area for the past 100-120 years.

Indonesia: 2010 Earthquake generated tsunami, 500 people killed, 22 active volcanoes.

Africa: Somalia: July 2011, the United Nations declared that the famine was worst in 60 years. 400,000 fled to **Ethiopia and Kenya**. The U.N. Refugee Agency expects to spend $997 million in the Horn of Africa because of famine and drought (Church News May 2012).

United States:

Hurricane Katrina (August 2005) It was the costliest natural disaster, as well as one of the five deadliest hurricanes, in the history of the United States. At least 1,833 died in the hurricane and subsequent floods. Total property damage was estimated at $81 billion (2005 USD).

Superstorm Sandy (October 2012) caused "widespread power outages and subway shutdowns... If the damages hit $50 billion, it would make Sandy the second-costliest U. S. storm after Katrina in 2005. Katrina's overall costs were $108 billion" (The Seattle Times November 2, 2012).

Tornadoes in U.S. Atlanta – 2011 One of the largest convulsions of tornado activity in U.S. History from Oklahoma to North Carolina and Virginia. Three day outbreak included 241 tornados reported over 14 states.

Joplin, Missouri – Deadliest twister on record. City of 50,000 wiped out. May 2011.

2011 The year of Disaster in U.S. Tornadoes, heat, fires, drought, floods, blizzards

The economic toll for extreme weather this year is estimated at $33 billion.

2012 – Drought disaster. The U.S. Department of Agriculture has declared 1,584 counties in 32 states, or 50.3 percent of all U.S. counties, disaster areas, mainly because of the drought (The Associated Press. August 2, 2012).

Worldwide Economic Cost of Disasters in 2011:

The highest in history with a price tag of at least $380 billion, mainly because of the earthquakes in Japan and New Zealand according to a U.N. envoy.

Prepare yourself, natural disasters will only get worse (The Washington Post, September 15, 2011).

"The world has entered a new era of catastrophes. Economic losses from hurricanes, earthquakes and resulting tsunamis, floods, wildfires and other natural disasters increased from $528 billion (1981-1990) to more than $1.2 trillion over the period 2001-2010. The 9.0 earthquake and massive tsunami in Japan this past spring caused hundreds of billions of dollars of direct and indirect costs. And before this, massive earthquakes in Haiti, Chile and New Zealand inflicted record human and financial losses as well."

United States of America – "The Land of the Free" (Free from what?)

Addictions:

Drugs - 22 million drug addicts in the United States and only 2 million get treatment.

Psychiatrists and other specialists are rewriting the manual that defines addiction, which could result in millions more people being diagnosed as addicts and pose huge consequences for health insurers and taxpayers (N.Y. Times, May 12, 2012).

"More babies born addicted to drugs" An increased reliance on prescription painkillers and the resulting addiction has now shown up in the most vulnerable patients–America's new-borns.

Addicted babies have nearly tripled in less than a decade. Average cost for the babies suffering from neonatal abstinence syndrome, increased from $39,400 to $53,400 between 2000 and 2009 (The Seattle Times May 1, 2012).

Alcohol: Alcohol is the number one drug problem in America.

Over 50 million Americans are dependent on alcohol. 500,000 are between the age of 9 and 12. Up to 40% of all industrial fatalities and 47% of industrial injuries can be linked to alcohol consumption.

Alcohol is involved in 50% of all driving fatalities. Alcohol and alcohol related problems is costing the American economy at least $100 million in health care and loss of productivity every year (Drug Rehabs.Org).

Gambling:

> "There is a legalized gambling avalanche in progress in America. The estimated cost is $50 billion a year. Gambling addiction leads to unemployment, bankruptcies, divorces, illnesses and sometimes suicides." (Sam Skolnik, Beacon Press).

Breakdown of the Family: Humanity has totally disregarded basic human values and morals. Especially, the breakdown of the family unit. Divorce and unwed motherhood is at an all-time high (MCT Internet Service – 1995)

The Decline of Marriage: As marriage has declined, cohabitation has become more widespread, nearly doubling since 1990, according to the Census Bureau. In the Pew Research Survey, 44% of all adults say they have cohabited at some point in their lives.

Divorce: The declining share of Americans who are currently married is fueled in large part by two big trends: The rise in the median age of first marriage and the increased prevalence of divorce (Pew Research Social and Demographic Trends, 2010).

Abortions There are more than one million abortions in the United States each year. From 2009-2011 estimates of 1,212,400 annually. (Alan Guttmacher Institute).

Aids Epidemic Continues: More than 1.8 million people in the U. S. are estimated to have been infected with HIV, including over 650,000 who have died (The Henry J. Kaiser Family Foundation, March 22, 2013).

More than 34 million people now live with HIV/AIDS worldwide (amFAR, Foundation for Aids Research, 2013).

APPENDIX 2

THE CREED OF ATHANASIUS

"We worship one God in Trinity, and Trinity in Unity, neither confounding the persons, nor dividing the substance. For there is one person of the Father, another of the Son, and another of the Holy Ghost. But the Godhead of the Father, Son, and Holy Ghost, is all one: the glory equal, the majesty co-eternal. Such as the Father is, such is the Son; and such is the Holy Ghost. The Father uncreate, the Son uncreate, and the Holy Ghost uncreate. The Father incomprehensible, the Son incomprehensible and the Holy Ghost incomprehensible. The Father eternal, the Son eternal, and the Holy Ghost eternal. And yet there are not three eternals; but one eternal. As also there are not three incomprehensibles, nor three uncreated; but one uncreated, and one incomprehensible. So likewise the Father is Almighty, the Son Almighty, and the Holy Ghost Almighty; and yet there are not three Almighties, but one Almighty. So the Father is God, the Son is God, and the Holy Ghost is God, and yet they are not three Gods but one God" (James E. Talmage, "The Great Apostasy" p. 104).

APPENDIX 3

SOME PAPAL HISTORY

"*O*n the death of Pope Paul I, who had attained the pontificate A.D. 757, the Duke of Nepi compelled some bishops to consecrate Constantine, one of his brothers, as pope; but more legitimate electors subsequently, A.D. 768, choosing Stephen IV, the usurper and his adherents were severely punished; the eyes of Constantine were put out; the tongue of the Bishop Theodorus was amputated, and he was left in a dungeon to expire in the agonies of thirst. The nephews of Pope Adrian seized his successor, Pope Leo III, A.D. 795, in the street, and, forcing him into a neighboring church, attempted to put out his eyes and cut out his tongue; at a later period, this pontiff, trying to suppress a conspiracy to depose him, Rome became the scene of rebellion, murder and conflagration. His successor, Stephen V, A.D. 816, was ignominiously driven from the city; his successor, Paschal I, was accused of blinding and murdering two ecclesiastics in the Lateran Palace; it was necessary that imperial commissioners should investigate the matter, but the pope died, after having exculpated himself by oath before thirty bishops.

John VIII A.D. 872, unable to resist the Mohammedans, was compelled to pay them tribute; the Bishop of Naples, maintaining a secret alliance with them, received his share of the plunder they collected. Him John excommunicated, nor would he give him absolution unless he would betray the chief Mohammedans and assassinate others himself. There was an ecclesiastical conspiracy to murder the pope; some of the treasures of the church were seized, and the gate of St. Pancrazia was opened with false keys, to admit the Saracens into the city. Formosus, who had been engaged in these transaction, and excommunicated as a conspirator for the murder of

John, was subsequently elected pope, A.D. 891; he was succeeded by Boniface VI, A.D. 896, who had been deposed from the diaconate, and again from the priesthood, for his immoral and lewd life. By Stephen VII, who followed, the dead body of Formosus was taken from the grave, clothed in the papal habiliments, propped up in a chair, tried before a council, and the preposterous and indecent scene completed by cutting off three of the fingers of the corpse and casting it into the Tiber; but Stephen himself was destined to exemplify how low the papacy had fallen: He was thrown into prison, and strangled.

In the course of five years, from A.D. 896 to A.D. 900, five popes were consecrated. Leo V, who succeeded in A.D. 904, was in less than two months thrown into prison by Christopher, one of his chaplains, who usurped his place, and who, in his turn, was shortly expelled from Rome by Sergius III, who, by the aid of a military force, seized the pontificate, A.D. 905. This man according to the testimony of the times, lived in criminal intercourse with the prostitute Theodora, who, with her daughters Marozia and Theodora, also prostitutes, exercised an extraordinary control over him. The love of Theodora was also shared by John X: she gave him first the archbishopric of Ravenna and then translated him to Rome, A.D. 915, as pope. John was not unsuited to the times; he organized a confederacy which perhaps prevented Rome from being captured by the Saracens, and the world was astonished and edified by the appearance of this war-like pontiff at the head of his troops. By the love of Theodora, as was said, he had maintained himself in the papacy for fourteen years; by the intrigues and hatred of her daughter Marozia he was overthrown. She surprised him in the Lateran Palace; killed his brother Peter before his face; threw him into prison, where he soon died, smothered, as was asserted, with a pillow. After a short interval Marozia, made her own son pope as John XI, A.D. 931. Many affirmed that Pope Sergius was his father, but she herself inclined to attribute him to her husband Alberic, whose brother Guido she subsequently married. Another of her sons, Alberic, so called from his supposed father, jealous of his brother John, cast him and their mother Marozia into prison. After a time Alberic's son was elected pope A.D. 956; he assumed the title of John XII, the amorous Marozia thus having given a son and a grandson to the papacy.

John was only nineteen years old when he thus became the head of Christendom. His rein was characterized by the most shocking immoralities, so that the Emperor Otho I was compelled by the German clergy to interfere. A synod was summoned for his trial in the Church of St. Peter, before which it appeared that John had received bribes for the consecration of bishops; that he had ordained one who was but ten years old, and had performed that ceremony over another in a stable; he was charged with incest with one his father's concubines, and with so many adulteries that the Lateran Palace had become a brothel; he put out the eyes of one ecclesiastic, and castrated another, both dying in consequence of their injuries; he was given to drunkenness, gambling and the invocation of Jupiter and Venus. When cited to appear before the council, he sent word that ' he had gone out hunting;' and to the fathers who remonstrated with him, he threateningly remarked 'that Judas, as well as the other disciples, received from his Master the power of binding and loosing, but that as soon as he proved a traitor to the common cause, the only power he retained was that of binding his own neck' Hereupon he was deposed, and Leo VIII elected in his stead, A.D. 963, but subsequently getting the upper hand, he seized his antagonists, cut off the hand of one, the nose, finger, tongue of others. His life was eventually brought to an end by the vengeance of a man whose wife he had seduced" (J. W. Draper, "Intellectual Development of Europe," Vol. I. Ch. XII, pp. 378-381).

APPENDIX 4

GOD RULES IN THE AFFAIRS OF MEN

"The will of God prevails. In great contests each party claims to act in accordance with the will of God. Both may be, and one must be, wrong. God cannot be for and against the same thing at the same time. In the present civil war it is quite possible that God's purpose is something different from the purpose of either party" (Nicolay and Hay, The Complete Works of Lincoln, 8:52-53).

"It is the duty of nations as well as of men to own their dependence upon the overruling power of God, to confess their sins and transgressions in humble sorrow, yet with assured hope that genuine repentance will lead to mercy and pardon, and to recognize the sublime truth, announced in the Holy Scriptures and proven by all history, that those nations only are blessed whose God is the Lord:

"And, insomuch as we know that by His divine law nations, like individuals, are subjected to punishments and chastisements in this world, may we not justly fear that the awful calamity of civil war which now desolates the land may be but a punishment inflicted upon us for our presumptuous sins, to the needful end of our national reformation as a whole people?

"We have been the recipients of the choicest bounties of Heaven; we have been preserved these many years in peace and prosperity. We have grown in numbers, wealth, and power, as no other nation has ever grown. **But we have forgotten God. We have forgotten the gracious hand which preserved us in peace and multiplied and enriched and strengthened us, and we have vainly imagined, in the deceitfulness of our hearts, that all these blessings were produced** by some superior wisdom and virtue of our own. Intoxicated with unbroken success, we have become too self-sufficient to feel the necessity of redeeming and preserving grace, too proud to pray to the God that made us.

"It behooves us, then, to humble ourselves before the Offended Power, to confess our national sins, and to pray for clemency and forgiveness" (Abraham Lincoln, "A Proclamation by the President of the United States of America. [a proclamation for a day of humiliation, fasting, and prayer." March 30, 1863], as cited in Richardson, Messages and Papers of the Presidents [Washington D.C.: United States Congress, 1897], pp. 164-65).

APPENDIX 5

THE TESTIMONY OF THREE WITNESSES TO THE BOOK OF MORMON

"Be it known unto all nations, kindreds, tongues, and people, unto whom this work shall come: That we, through the grace of God the Father, and our Lord Jesus Christ, have seen the plates which contain this record, which is a record of the people of Nephi, and also of the Lamanites, their brethren, and also of the people of Jared, who came from the tower of which hath been spoken. And we also know that they have been translated by the gift and power of God, for his voice hath declared it unto us; wherefore we know of a surety that the work is true. And we also testify that we have seen the engravings which are upon the plates; and they have been shown unto us by the power of God, and not of man. And we declare with words of soberness, that an angel of God came down from heaven, and he brought and lade before our eyes, that we beheld and saw the plates, and the engravings thereon; and we know that it is by the grace of God the Father, and our Lord Jesus Christ, that we beheld and bear record that these things are true. And it is marvelous in our eyes. Nevertheless, the voice of the Lord commanded us that we should bear record of it; wherefore, to be obedient unto the commandments of God, we bear testimony of these things. And we know that if we are faithful in Christ, we shall rid our garments of the blood of all men, and be found spotless before the judgment-seat of Christ, and shall dwell with him eternally in the heavens. And the honor be to the Father, and to the Son, and to the Holy Ghost, which is one God. Amen."

Oliver Cowdery, David Whitmer, Martin Harris

APPENDIX 6

THE FAMILY
A PROCLAMATION TO THE WORLD

We, the First Presidency and the Council of the Twelve Apostles of The Church of Jesus Christ of Latter-day Saints, solemnly proclaim that marriage between a man and a woman is ordained of God and that the family is central to the Creator's plan for the eternal destiny of His children.

All human beings–male and female–are created in the image of God. Each is a beloved spirit son or daughter of heavenly parents, and, as such, each has a divine nature and destiny. Gender is an essential characteristic of individual premortal, mortal, and eternal identity and purpose.

In the premortal realm, spirit sons and daughters knew and worshipped God as their Eternal Father and accepted His plan by which His children could obtain a physical body and gain earthly experience to progress toward perfection and ultimately realize his or her divine destiny as an heir of eternal life. The divine plan of happiness enables family relationships to be perpetuated beyond the grave. Sacred ordinances and covenants available in holy temples make it possible for individuals to return to the presence of God and for families to be united eternally.

The first commandment that God gave to Adam and Eve pertained to their potential for parenthood as husband and wife. We declare that God's commandment for His children to multiply and replenish the earth remains in force. We further declare that God has commanded that the sacred powers of procreation are to be employed only between man and woman, lawfully wedded as husband and wife.

We declare the means by which mortal life is created to be divinely appointed. We affirm the sanctity of life and of its importance in God's eternal plan.

Husband and wife have a solemn responsibility to love and care for each other and for their children. "Children are an heritage of the Lord" (Psalms 127:3). Parents have a sacred duty to rear their children in love and righteousness, to provide for their physical and spiritual needs, to teach them to love and serve one another, to observe the commandments of God and to be law-abiding citizens wherever they live. Husbands and wives—mothers and fathers—will be held accountable before God for the discharge of these obligations.

The family is ordained of God. Marriage between man and woman is essential to His eternal plan. Children are entitled to birth within the bonds of matrimony, and to be reared by a father and a mother who honor marital vows with complete fidelity. Happiness in family life is most likely to be achieved when founded upon the teachings of the Lord Jesus Christ. Successful marriages and families are established and maintained on principles of faith, prayer, repentance, forgiveness, respect, love, compassion, work, and wholesome recreational activities. By divine design, fathers are to preside over their families in love and righteousness and are responsible to provide the necessities of life and protection for their families. Mothers are primarily responsible for the nurture of their children. In these sacred responsibilities, fathers and mothers are obligated to help one another as equal partners. Disability, death, or other circumstances may necessitate individual adaptation. Extended families should lend support when needed.

We warn that individuals who violate covenants of chastity, who abuse spouse or offspring, or who fail to fulfill family responsibilities will one day stand accountable before God. Further, we warn that the disintegration of the family will bring upon individuals, communities, and nations the calamities foretold by ancient and modern prophets.

We call upon responsible citizens and officers of government everywhere to promote those measures designed to maintain and strengthen the family as the fundamental unit of society.